In the future—after many of us Baby Boomers are dead and buried—Nyren's book could well be hailed as a classic in the annals of advertising education. Looking back, some may call him a pundit. Others may call him a visionary. Both would be correct. In my opinion [the book] is a "must read" for any executives who wonder which half of their advertising dollars is being wasted.

—**Eric Voth**, ERV Productions

I bought over 80 books on the subject of Boomers, advertising, and marketing for my M.A. thesis on images of Boomer women. Chuck Nyren was the only writer who put it all together, brilliantly, in one source. His book was the mainstay of my citations. Any advertiser who does not understand his premise that Boomers are diverse adults who do not want to be seen as Steve Martin's caricature of "wild and crazy guys" is going to alienate this pivotal generation—or, worse yet, miss them all together.

—**Mary Duffy**, Ford Models, 40+ fashion and beauty writer

Chuck Nyren's wit and charm only partially disguise the razor-sharp teeth that he flashes at an industry in denial.

—**Marc Middleton,** founder and president, The Growing Bolder Media Group

If you get the idea that you need to reach baby boomers, Chuck's book is the foundation for that effort.

—**Jon Currie,** Currie Communications

Chuck Nyren is a funny writer. Well, he's a serious writer who's funny. Since everyone is trying to figure out how to market to Baby Boomers, his book will probably be the best guide yet.

—**Jan Reisen,** *AgingHipsters.com*

I like the way [Nyren] seems, between the lines, to be giving us boomers our dignity back.

—**Julie Muhlstein**, *The Everett Herald*

Advertising to Baby Boomers unlocks the minds and hearts of the large and affluent generation that challenged the reconfigured society's rules at each stage of life. . . . Nyren is serious about his precepts, but easy to read and humorous in his writing style . . . even the most experienced professionals are likely to hit upon new ideas for increasing their products' appeal among boomer market consumers.

—Excerpted from *GenerationTarget.com*

MARKETING BOOKS FROM PMP

MARKET RESEARCH

The 4Cs of Truth in Communication: *How to Identify, Discuss, Evaluate, and Present Stand-out, Effective Communication*

Consumer Insights 2.0: *How Smart Companies Apply Customer Knowledge to the Bottom Line*

Dominators, Cynics, and Wallflowers: *Practical Strategies for Moderating Meaningful Focus Groups*

Moderating to the Max! *A Full-Tilt Guide to Creative, Insightful Focus Groups and Depth Interviews*

The Mirrored Window: *Focus Groups from a Moderator's Point of View*

Religion in a Free Market: *Religious and Non-Religious Americans—Who, What, Why, Where*

Why People Buy Things They Don't Need

MATURE MARKET/ BABY BOOMERS

After Fifty: *How the Baby Boom Will Redefine the Mature Market*

After Sixty: *Marketing to Baby Boomers Reaching Their Big Transition Years*

Advertising to Baby Boomers

Marketing to Leading-Edge Baby Boomers

The Boomer Heartbeat: *Capturing the Heartbeat of the Baby Boomers Now and in the Future*

MULTICULTURAL

Beyond Bodegas: *Developing a Retail Relationship with Hispanic Customers*

Hispanic Marketing Grows Up: *Exploring Perceptions and Facing Realities*

Marketing to American Latinos: *A Guide to the In-Culture Approach, Part I*

Marketing to American Latinos: *A Guide to the In-Culture Approach, Part II*

The Whole Enchilada: *Hispanic Marketing 101*

What's Black About It? *Insights to Increase Your Share of a Changing African-American Market*

YOUTH MARKETS

The Kids Market: *Myths & Realities*

Marketing to the New Super Consumer: Mom & Kid

The Great Tween Buying Machine: *Marketing to Today's Tweens*

MARKETING MANAGEMENT

A Clear Eye for Branding: *Straight Talk on Today's Most Powerful Business Concept*

A Knight's Code of Business: *How to Achieve Character and Competence in the Corporate World*

Beyond the Mission Statement: *Why Cause-Based Communications Lead to True Success*

India Business: *Finding Opportunities in this Big Emerging Market*

Marketing Insights to Help Your Business Grow

Advertising to Baby Boomers

REVISED & UPDATED

Chuck Nyren

PARAMOUNT MARKET PUBLISHING, INC.

Paramount Market Publishing, Inc.
950 Danby Road, Suite 136
Ithaca, NY 14850
www.paramountbooks.com
Telephone: 607-275-8100; 888-787-8100   Facsimile: 607-275-8101

Publisher: James Madden
Editorial Director: Doris Walsh

ISBN-10: 0-9786602-3-4
ISBN-13: 978-0-9786602-3-9

This book is dedicated to my favorite copywriter,

GAYLE SCHWINN NYREN (1925–1994)

CONTENTS

ACKNOWLEDGEMENTS

BREVITY RULES HERE, or this could go on for pages. For now my thanks to: mostly Jill, Clifford, and Stuart for their support above and beyond the call of sibling duty; Gary, Darla, and Tamara; Ashley and Morgan, my two brightest, prettiest stars; David O. Nyren, Dancer, Fitzgerald & Sample's "face" in the late Fifties and Sixties; Sid Schwinn, the family advertising patriarch; Brent Green for introducing me not to advertising, not to Baby Boomers, but to such a potent blend; Mary Furlong, the Queen of movers and shakers; John Migliaccio, my blues brother; the folks at Suite101.com for putting up with me; Ron Koliha for being there by rarely being there; Jef I. Richards although he has no idea who I am, but he saved me hours and hours of manually highlighting and typing; Doris Walsh for chuckling and cutting (or at least cutting); Tika, although she knows nothing about this; Sue & Jeff at DPS; most of my clients; and Patricia, who is and will always be "the best."

PREFACE TO THE SECOND EDITION

THE FIRST EDITION of this book was published in June 2005. Copies ended up in the hands of some influential folk thanks to Paramount Market Publishing and Len Stein of Visibility PR.

There was one outcome I wasn't ready for: *Advertising to Baby Boomers* was selected as a classroom resource by The Advertising Educational Foundation. Only thirty or so books have been selected as classroom resources by AEF out of thousands of marketing and advertising books released each year.

I was shocked, flattered, and obviously honored. *Advertising to Baby Boomers* isn't exactly an academic treatise. It's been described by many as a bold, breezy read, often polemical, a rant, with humorous asides and potent advice nestled between shrieks.

Since then, hundreds of college and university libraries around the world have scooped it up. I receive a steady stream of emails and phone calls from students and professors. Not a typical one, but a fun one:

> To: Chuck Nyren
> From: (A professor at a university in Pennsylvania)
> Subject: Keep Preachin'
>
> Keep preachin' brother because some still refuse to hear. My students just presented a campaign geared to baby boomers to a group of judges at the National Student Advertising Competition. When we mentioned your book as proof that boomers don't like flashy ads, some 25-year-old copywriter/judge from BBDO West told them, "I can't believe boomers don't like slick ads." So, keep preachin' and maybe they too will one day hear.

In August 2005 I was a guest on *Advertising Age*'s syndicated radio program *The Advertising Show*, where I mixed it up with industry pros Brad Forsythe and Ray Schilens. Again, lots of fun and an honor to have been invited. Then came a bunch of positive reviews, dozens of interviews in newspapers, magazines, and on radio, and offers to write pieces for trade mags, web sites, and advertising agency newsletters. I've spoken at many summits and conferences around the country. I just keep preachin'.

But the bigger story is all the press Baby Boomers are receiving lately. Technically, the first Baby Boomer turned 60 years old in January 2006. *Newsweek, Businessweek, MSNBC,* and dozens of media outlets have had special reports about this unwieldy generation and its non-stop influence on just about everything. Conventional wisdom says that this influence will continue for at least another 25 years.

And shock of shocks, the advertising industry is beginning to acknowledge this demographic. However, I'm not so sure that they are doing an adequate job with their marketing and creative campaigns. I talked about this in the first edition, and expand on it in this edition.

The victims, of course, are advertisers. Most are not getting their money's worth. The lessons about marketing and advertising to Baby Boomers in this book and a handful of others have yet to be put to good use.

About This Edition

Five chapters have been punched up and updated. There are a handful of fresh chapters. Most of the new material was inspired by the dozens of people I've met over the last year and a half: other advertising and marketing folk, clients who have come aboard for consulting and creative work, professors and students eager to learn from me (but I end up learning more from them). What great company I've been keeping.

Write a business book sometime. You'll think that you've said it all. Then people read it, you make friends, you discuss the themes in your book, they have their own ideas and opinions about it all—and you're humbled a hundred times over.

—CHUCK NYREN
January 2007

"No, I don't think a 68-year-old copywriter . . . can write with the kids. That he's as creative. That he's as fresh. But he may be a better surgeon. His ad may not be quite as fresh and glowing as the Madison Avenue fraternity would like to see it be, and yet he might write an ad that will produce five times the sales. And that's the name of the game, isn't it?"

—Rosser Reeves

The Geritol Syndrome

IF YOU'RE A BABY BOOMER you remember the early television ads for Geritol™ (*"Do you have iron-poor, tired blood?"*). They were dry, stilted, and among kids fidgeting in front of the box, often evoked laughter.

One from the Fifties had a husband coming home to a messy house and an apathetic wife. He pulls out a pistol and pulls the trigger. Out pops a banner, unfurling the word "Geritol." The next day the house is clean, the wife perky.

Others were more dramatic. The plots for these one-minute soap operas went something like this: A mother or grandmother was tired, irritable. A husband would notice—and with concern, lovingly comment. Sage advice followed. The message: A daily spoonful of Geritol saves marriages. One memorable tag line was: "*My wife. I think I'll keep her.*"

Today the Geritol spots are considered an anathema when discussing 50-plus marketing. You could use them as examples of what *not* to do. But no one talks about how effective they were in reaching their target market. As usual, the truth lies somewhere in between. The Geritol campaigns were successful because of their simple, direct messages. A similar campaign today, using vague, anxiety-ridden scare tactics, might not work for Baby Boomers. We're too smart (or perhaps too jaded) to be fooled by hackneyed situations and simplistic answers.

However, this doesn't mean that a clear, direct message about your product or service would not be effective. The real reason the Geritol ads were funny was because they weren't exactly the cutting-edge of advertising "art." These weren't *sexy* ads, ones that an agency would brandish as their best work. Over martinis just off Madison Avenue, I doubt that you ever heard, "Wow! Did you see the latest Geritol spot? Baby, *fantabulous!*"

And so continues the Geritol Syndrome. When advertisers *do* "get creative" and target Baby Boomers, they're usually off the mark. The spot for Cadillac using Led Zeppelin's "Rock and Roll" oozes cognitive dissonance, but after an initial jump in sales, the commercial is now considered a flop. The campaign was revamped, keeping the music (snippets of the guitar breaks, none of this "Been a long time since I rock 'n' rolled"), and are now targeted to a younger demographic.

Too bad; they probably could have done better.

Then there are the prescription drug ads, like the one with Boomer pod people standing motionless on some sci-fi planet, eerily announcing, one-by-one, how they feel better after . . . I don't know . . . after becoming pod people.

"Baby, fantabulous!"

To be fair, it's not always the agency's fault. Clients often have some vague notion of what they want, and the balancing act isn't always easy, or successful. Do you create a campaign for the client or for the public? This is a familiar-to-ad agencies dilemma.

But if Cadillac wants to appeal to Baby Boomers (we think of Cads as cars gangsters drive, or as hearses) do you really have to position them as something that will make us feel young again as we zoom around blasting rock and roll while our car is in cruise control? Only occasionally do we sit around and daydream about being eighteen again. Most of the time we don't feel that old.

To promote prescription drugs (or almost anything) must you use overblown computer graphics to create some visually demented atmosphere that looks like the latest video game? I think not.

Personally, I often get a chuckle out of computer morphing and all the latest special effects (although they're getting old fast). And I don't mind being entertained with witty turns-of-phrase. But Baby Boomers have seen it all. We grew up watching commercials.

You can amuse, but don't assume. Give us the facts. Pitching to the emotions instead of the brain is the biggest mistake agencies make when marketing and advertising to Baby Boomers.* We'll decide for ourselves how fast to take the curves in our new Caddies.

> * Actually, there are ways of "pitching to the emotions" of Baby Boomers (emotional branding). The problem is that advertising agencies more often than not pitch to the wrong emotions—and there's a reason why. I'll talk about this later.

We'll also decide a few other things before long, including how, when, and where we will be marketed to. The ubiquity of the worldwide web and cable television, the ease and affordability of computer printing of magazines and books, along with other forms of communication are creating new ways of reaching all demographics. But it will be the Baby Boomers who will be the first to pick and choose, to ignore or be seduced by leading-edge technology marketing.

There's a simple reason for this. *We have the money to buy this stuff.* Experts say we'll continue to have the money for at least the next twenty years. Write us off at your own peril.

So What Are the Target Markets for this Book?

Let's work from the bottom up:

Tertiary: On the surface, it might seem that *Advertising to Baby Boomers* is a "how-to" for major advertising agencies and multi-national marketing firms, the big guys.

I'm sure they'll get something out of it. According to internet stats from various websites I write for, they already have, downloading and printing many of my articles over the last few years.

But corporations are hulking behemoths, not amenable to new ideas or sweeping changes. I'm proposing a minor revolution in the advertising industry, one that won't trickle down but bubble up. It's not a technology driven revolution. It's a human one.

Secondary: Small-to-medium-sized advertising and marketing agencies. They may squirm at first, even kick and scream—but eventually will be co-beneficiaries of this common sense revolution. Some may become the heroes and heroines of this reasoned paradigm.

Primary: It's a book about advertising—but I've written it for any-body who owns or works for a company—large, medium, or small—and is involved with marketing a product or service where one of your target markets is (or should be) the 40-plus demographic. Even though it comes from a creative advertising perspective, this book is *for the client.*

When targeting Baby Boomers, I'm not convinced that the advertising industry is serving its clients well. You're not getting your money's worth. Some simple demands, a bit of vigilance, and you could change things around, and get *much more* than you're paying for.

Advertising to Baby Boomers is also for anybody with a marketing or product idea, yet to be realized or about to come to market. Venture capitalists take heed: the largest demographic of entrepreneurs are over forty, the largest consumer demographic the same. Baby Boomers will soon be marketing to themselves again, after a hiatus of twenty-odd years.

What's to Be Gleaned from These Pages

If this is a "how-to" book, it's how to effectively communicate and partner with an advertising agency or creative freelancer.

- How to find a good one for your product or service, one that understands on an instinctive level how to communicate with the 40-plus market.
- What questions you should ask when interviewing or being "pitched" by an agency.
- How to help develop a campaign with your agency.
- When to step in with advice and demands, and when to leave them alone.
- When to trust the advertising or marketing agency, and when to question its judgments.
- How to demand more from your ad agency when building campaigns aimed at Baby Boomers.
- How to critique ad campaigns.

I'm not leaving out the small entrepreneur with the bullets above. Many examples I provide, comments I make, and ideas I propose focus on advertising campaigns and products with which you are probably familiar. Don't be intimidated. The advertising principles are the same for General Motors worldwide as they are for a General Store in a semi-retirement or vacation community.

Or you may have a flair for writing, for graphics, for marketing and selling. If you've developed that better mousetrap and you are marketing it, on eBay or anywhere else, *Advertising to Baby Boomers* may spark some ideas of your own. Use this book as a starting point for your handmade campaign.

I'll also be causing some trouble, ruffling feathers. (I already have, if you haven't noticed.) But the purpose of this book is to get your brain roiling and place you on track when you're focusing on advertising to this specific market and its cohorts. If you think I'm off the mark every so often (or even often), fine. If what comes out of this are better ideas of your own, then as far as I'm concerned *Advertising to Baby Boomers* has served its purpose.

That's what this book really is: a catalyst for creative thinking.

And, if you're a businessperson, you know that creative thinking doesn't begin and end inside an advertising agency.

PART I

Some Guidelines for Boomer Advertising

CHAPTER ONE

Why Companies and Ad Agencies Need Baby Boomers

> Boomers have transformed American society and institutions, but not always in ways they had anticipated or like to remember . . . Boomers control most major institutions in America . . . the ethic of self-fulfillment and the broader definition of individualism have seeped into every corner of American society and culture. . . . Their emphasis on individual rights and the underlying challenge to authority led to a dramatic democratization of American culture. . . . Today, Boomer culture is American culture.
>
> —Steve Gillon, *Boomer Nation*[1]

THIS BOOK IS NOT A "WHO DUNNIT?" It's a business book. If there is a mystery to unravel, I'll lay it all out in front of you before the end of this chapter. It's also not a pedantic history book—but stick with me for a bit.

Advertising and marketing weren't always as complicated as they are today. For various reasons (cultural, economic, political) many demographic groups were completely ignored. The conventional (and unspoken) wisdom was, "Why market to them? We reach them and they have to buy products anyway. So why sully our ads with non-white folks, except as comic foils?"

Without too much debate, you could pretty much break down targeted demographics in the first decades of the 20th century this way:

---

1 Steve Gillon, *Boomer Nation: The Largest and Richest Generation Ever, and How It Changed America* (New York: Free Press, 2004)

- Young
- Old
- Male
- Female
- Rich
- Middle Class
- City
- Country

. . . and all White.

Mix and match for cohorts.

If I were to make a list of all the markets and their cohorts today it would go on for ten pages. There are hundreds of marketing books for hundreds of identified demographics, numerous books for each cohort within these markets.

Things have changed, all for the better—culturally and economically. However, a strange thing happened during this constructive inclusion of targeted social groups. Each generation of advertisers developed its own versions of yesteryear's myopia and conceit.

While advertising agencies were never a healthy blend of gender and ethnicity until recently (and many still believe quite correctly that it isn't quite perfect yet), agencies of the past were usually an effective mixture of young, middle-aged, and old. Creative directors, copywriters, and graphic artists could be any age. Smart account execs assigned accounts to creatives based on their age and cultural strengths.

Of course, it was tough to assign creatives based on their ages and cultural strengths if your target market wore diapers or shot spitballs out of straws. But after World War II they did what they could as babies were being born by the millions.

That would be the Baby Boomers (and would include Yours Truly). Because of our numbers, we were bunched together and ruthlessly targeted beginning in the early Fifties. The toy business turned into big business. Upon becoming teenagers in the late Fifties and early Sixties, we were still trusting, non-judgmental marketing fodder.

But something happened in the middle- and late-Sixties. Ad agencies started to get it wrong. Cultural revolutions were happening in and around their precious Baby Boomer target market, and things became a bit chaotic and very confusing. Whether we as individuals jumped into the fray or not, took sides or not, didn't matter. We were affected. And we weren't buying into much of what Madison Avenue was offering. Out-of-touch adults weren't reaching us.

> When future historians look back at the contribution made by the Boomer generation, they will no doubt place the expansion of individual freedom at the top of the list of achievements. Boomers not only cheered on the civil rights movement, they spearheaded the feminist cause in the 1970s, and fought for a host of new rights and responsibilities—not just gay rights, handicapped rights, the right to privacy, but the responsibility of everyone to participate in the economy, or more generally just to become engaged in the culture—that changed the tone and character of modern life.
>
> —Steve Gillon, *Boomer Nation*

Partly to save their hides, ad agencies turned their creative departments over to twenty-somethings. The sheer size of Baby Boomers made them *the* market—composed of scores of unwieldy cohorts. By attrition, this would have occurred naturally. It just happened ten or fifteen years sooner than with previous generations coming of age.

Barely out of college, Baby Boomers were in control of marketing and advertising to themselves—and became successful at it. After all, we knew the market.

Most of the advertising campaigns were pure gut, spiked with brash creativity. Not much studying of unfamiliar demographics required. Just being *young* was enough. You could slice and dice the cohorts if you had nothing better to do—but the common denominator was that we were all in our late teens to early thirties (that infamous 18–34 age bracket). We were all young. Market and advertise to *that*. Whites, African-Americans, Latinos, Asians—all young. What else did we need to know?

Boomers were the largest demographic, the primary target. Conventional wisdom: "All others (kids, older people) were simply niche markets. Why market to them? Besides, we reach older folks and they have to buy products anyway. So why sully our ads with old people and kids, except as comic foils?" (Think *Mr. Whipple*, "*Where's the beef?*" *Rodney Allan Rippy, Mikey*)

But over the last fifteen years, two concurrent cultural revolutions have happened. They weren't as dramatic as the ones of the Sixties, but the repercussions have been and will be profound.

The first was the breakup of mass media. Not of the ownership—those battles are still being fought in and around the FCC. This "breakup" had to do with the multitudinous choices we now have for information and entertainment.

We don't all watch the same three television stations anymore. We don't all read the same newspapers and magazines (on the internet or in print). Media outlets have grown exponentially, and have their own audience "cohorts."

I'll leave this first revolution alone. It bleeds into the next, but is not the subject of this book. There are many excellent ones that deal with media and multi-cultural marketing.

The second very slow, imperceptible revolution had to do with age. That huge, seemingly amorphous group, those irrepressible Baby Boomers, kept getting older. We're now in our forties and fifties.

Due to our sheer numbers, and because we expanded and kept the economy thriving through our twenties and thirties, Baby Boomers are now the richest generation in history. Not all of us—but as a whole. We continue to be *the* most powerful, influential socio-economic group.

> This big and growing over-45 segment of the population is also the most affluent. Collectively, those 46 and older control more than half of the nation's discretionary income.
>
> —*The New York Times*[2]

2 Gilpin, Kenneth, "Selling to 45-Plus Generation: That's Where the Money Is," *The New York Times*, December 1, 2003

By 2005, 38 million boomers will be 50 or older. While mature Americans make up 35 percent of the population, they have more than 75 percent of the financial assets and nearly 60 percent of the discretionary income. In the marketplace, that makes them the 800-pound gorilla.

—The Hartford Courant[3]

According to data collected by the U.S. Census and Federal Reserve, the 78 million Americans who were 50 or older as of 2001 controlled $28 trillion, or 67% of the country's wealth.

—Brent Green, *Advertising and Marketing Review*[4]

Along the way, there was a major marketing disconnect. We're still the largest and richest demographic—but as far as advertising agencies are concerned, we're off the radar.

How did this happen?

Baby Boomers who worked in the advertising industry have moved on; partly by choice, partly by design. In many cases we've been kicked out or kicked upstairs. Natural attrition. It was meant to be. It's the normal course of events.

We have left a positive and important legacy in the marketing and advertising worlds: racial and ethnic inclusion, lifestyle inclusion, tons more perceived markets.

But we also left advertising agencies the "Youth Culture."

The conventional wisdom today: "Why market to Baby Boomers? We reach them anyway. And they have to buy products anyway. So why sully our ads with middle-aged folks, except as comic foils?"

We taught them too well.

Advertising agencies are image-conscious and want to be "hip" (again, residue from Baby Boomers). Not only do they *not* want to market to Baby Boomers—they simply want to do what they do best: *market to themselves.* They certainly don't want to be known as an agency that markets to "older folks" (The Geritol Syndrome).

Again, we taught them too well.

---

3 "Boomers Influence Home Products, *Hartford Courant,* April 6, 2004.

4 Green, Brent, "Boomers: Toward a Higher Marketing Consciousness," *Advertising & Marketing Review,* June 2004.

So you don't think this chapter is completely self-serving: A few years ago I was approached by a small company that produced video games. I pretty much said to them, "Why are you interested in me doing creative strategy and copywriting? I'm fifty-one. Find an ad agency that has some young copywriters who know more about these types of products, understand the youth culture today, and can really write and advertise to your market." And I sent them to a couple of small local ad agencies.

The point is, when marketing and advertising to Baby Boomers, don't trust anybody under forty.

Unfortunately, you won't find too many people *over* forty in advertising agencies.

The Elephant in the Room

I've simplified things to make some points. They are valid points, however. I've also bundled Baby Boomers with various social and ethnic groups, possibly giving the impression that we have become "victims" like they once were (and some still are). Nothing could be further from the truth. I simply want to explain why advertising agencies now consider us invisible. But we're more than simply invisible. We're the elephant in the room that everybody ignores. Actually, we're the *Cash Cow* everybody ignores. Big mistake.

Again, straining the definition of "victim," who *are* the victims?

Baby Boomers? Not at all. We've done okay for ourselves. Like all generations we've achieved a great deal, fell short in some ways and because we're still an active bunch we have many more chances to achieve, more chances to fail. Our history is far from being written.

Advertising agencies? A trillion-dollar industry is not a victim. They're just bloated, satisfied, and because nobody is pushing them to change, they're sitting pretty.

The "victims" are the tens of thousands of companies, large and small, who have products and services for the consumer market. When a company hires an advertising agency, it's a good bet that they are *not* getting their money's worth.

The Giant Leap

Today's advertising industry needs a minor revolution. Talented men and women in their forties and fifties need to be brought back into the fold if you want to reach Baby Boomers. This includes account executives, copywriters, graphic artists, producers, directors, creative directors. If you plan on implementing a marketing strategy that includes Baby Boomers as a primary, secondary, or tertiary market, and you turn it over to a different generation of advertising professionals, you will forfeit the natural sensibilities required to generate vital campaigns.

Truth is, you can analyze marketing fodder all day and night, read countless books about marketing to Baby Boomers, attend advertising and marketing conventions around the world, and soak up everything all the experts have to say. Much of what is out there is valuable and useful. Some is required reading (I'll talk about a few later on in chapter twenty. But the bottom line is this: If the right people aren't in the right jobs—well, you know what happens. What happens is what happens in all arenas of business: failure and (sometimes even worse) mediocrity.

"They buy products anyway . . . "

Sure "they" do. But do they buy *your* products instead of the competition's?

Advertising agencies write off *your potential target market* because they don't know how to advertise to Baby Boomers anymore than I know how to reach a teenager or young adult who wriggles and zigzags around in his or her chair, punching, skidding, and spastically rattling something I believe is referred to as a *joystick*.

Older generations used this term for something never mentioned in mainstream ads.* Baby Boomers used this term for something a former President didn't inhale. Don't try to sell *me* a joystick; I will be either severely disappointed with your product, or I will make a citizen's arrest.

* Well, guess how it *is* being mentioned.

As I've said, the middle-aged blood has moved on. They've become top execs, have retired, or are now employed in other industries.

How do you get them back? Do they want to get their hands dirty again? These former crackerjack creatives *must* be convinced that they are needed. As a client, you must demand that the right people work on the right campaigns.

Here's an e-mail I received:

Chuck,

Very interesting concepts regarding the marketing to Baby Boomers . . . I enjoy your writing style . . .

I am an American . . . who was transferred to Sydney, Australia in 1981 by [a very large ad agency] and never looked back. Over the next twenty years I raised a family, ran agencies (including my own) in Sydney, Singapore and Malaysia. . . .

Now I am looking at returning to Los Angeles to be closer to my origins and family and am considering the direction of my new venture in LA . . . I have felt for some years that the majority of leading advertising agencies and companies either disregard Boomers totally or only give scant consideration to what is the single most vibrant and exciting consumer group in the world. And this is a problem in Australia as well as the USA. . . .

Outside of the typical categories appealing to Boomers (real estate investment, travel, financial services) the majority of companies and agencies simply don't make the effort. And I think they do so at their own peril. . . .

I come from an Account Management/Strategic Planning background so my copy is nothing like yours but I believe my experience is ideally suited to developing marketing to Boomers . . .

So, my question is, how do I get back into the game in LA in this capacity after being away since 1981? I've got the credentials, passion and drive to make it happen . . .

Appreciate any thoughts you might have. . . .

—Bill D.

I have thoughts, but they're not pretty ones.

As a company with almost any product or service to offer, does this fellow seem like someone whom you might want to handle your advertising account? Or at the very least generate valuable professional input and be "on the team"?

Advertising agencies don't think so.

The best advertisers are advertisers who advertise to themselves.

Quality Control

It's going to be up to companies to be proactive when dealing with advertising agencies. Quality control of your product doesn't stop at the entrances of Madison Avenue's finest, or at the doors of small local or regional advertising agencies.

If companies put pressure on agencies, and demand 45–plus creatives for products aimed at the 45–plus market, then they will find out that Baby Boomers are still *"the single most vibrant and exciting consumer group in the world."*

CHAPTER TWO

Make the Most of the Boomer Market

GENERATIONAL ADVERTISING is not about rules. It's about defining playing fields. Baby Boomers who are, or were once, in the advertising industry know the rules already, and (I hope) have bent, twisted, mutilated, and unceremoniously chucked most of them.

I won't be dispensing dreary litanies of facts and figures, sure-fire promotional schemes, or new-age marketing meditation techniques that promise to magically invoke caboodles of Baby Boomers cloying at your product or salivating over your service.

I'm simply interested in educating companies with Baby Boomers as a target market, and talking a bit about what goes on in the creative department of an ad agency (large or small) so you can keep an eye on them. *You are in charge*, and *you* have to know the rules so you can allow copywriters and designers to break them, but not go too far afield.

The Baby Boomers Ballpark is more than simply an admixture of large fonts, penetrating and inclusive copy, fresh unfettered graphics, and messages that are declarative and free of empty slogans.

In fact, the word "slogan" isn't used much anymore in the industry. Slogans are now "corporate tags" or "branding idioms" or "image drivers" or something equally pretentious. Make sure that when a copywriter comes up with one for your product it isn't just fluff (or age-related). I'll talk more about this in a later chapter.

Within this framework, let them go wild.

That's because the blandness of most 50-plus advertising of the past won't work for Baby Boomers. We appreciate a witty turn of phrase, a humorous slant on things, even slightly skewed personas dramatized or pitching products. *Just make sure the wit isn't derogatory, the humor isn't embarrassing, and the personas aren't doddering.*

Fear and anxiety are not generation-specific, but personality-specific. Many Baby Boomers scoff at overt fear mongering, while others respond to the "fear factor." To capture both groups (and all the in-betweens), you might be better off focusing solely on the products or services, not the possible horrors of being without "it." There are plenty of rational reasons for purchasing insurance, security services, and medical products.

Let me overstate this to make my point: we don't need to "see" houses burning, burglars ransacking, or people tipping over from heart attacks or hay fever. Even alluding to these things will either be snickered at, or trigger fearful thoughts that may take your reader or viewer off into the anxious ether, obscuring your message, and, more than likely, your product.

Stick to the solution, not the problem.

While many of the recent television spots for prescription pills are a bit spacey and not always effective, at least they do a good job of not dwelling on the negative. Take heed. *Give your agency parameters, not rules.* Let your ad agency break or make up its own rules.

Using Humor in Campaigns

Creatives can come up with plenty of amusing scenarios that don't rely on age-related foibles. People are funny at all ages, and often for the same reasons. The easiest target is usually the least creative, and always the least effective way of delivering a potent message.

As a fiction and non-fiction writer, I rarely censor my pieces. There are no sacred cows. Something has to be *really* politically incorrect for me to lay off.

However, there are rules and constructs when using humor in advertising. I try to break and ignore as many as I can whenever I can, but I have no problems working within a self-imposed, acceptable framework when fashioning copy and a campaign. Advertising is artsy, but it isn't art.

As important as your target market is, it's just as important not to alien-ate secondary and hidden markets. Advertising campaigns, and the prod-ucts and services promoted, often take on lives of their own, appealing to market segments you may never have considered.

For example, there's a very funny television commercial for a web-based hotel/vacation service. I believe the campaign began with a spot whose tongue-in-cheek message was, "Take your teenagers with you or they'll throw wild parties and wreck your house." The subsequent spot had a wife in her early thirties looking for the perfect vacation. She impulsively clicks a link to hotels that offer "natural surround-ings." Up pops a picture of a beautiful hut-like cabin on a South Sea island. How romantic, she imagines.

Then her fantasy turns to horror. She and her husband are in a bed covered with a mosquito net, and they wake up screaming. The net is covered with hundreds of large, wriggly insects. If not glued to the net, the creatures are flying around the room.

Breaking out of her nightmare, she clicks on a list of hotels that aren't quite as exotic.

It's as perfect a commercial as you'll find. While the actors are in their early thirties, not a person alive would have a problem relating to the wife's fears and apprehensions. I'm sure folks in their sixties or seventies likewise found the commercial funny and could relate to it. The spot would've worked had the actors have been any age. That's because the principal was gently poking fun at herself.

The follow-up spot in the campaign was a dud. I'm sure the cre-ative powers-that-be didn't want to repeat the "plot," so they racked their brains for a different angle. They failed miserably, and in the process alienated secondary market segments.

This time, a woman in her early thirties (it may have been the same actress) is looking for the perfect hotel for her parents. She clicks on a link to "ultra-modern." Her horror fantasy begins. We see her parents in a Jetsons-like hotel room. The father is a bit wary of a space-age chair, finally decides to take the plunge, the chair tips over, and he tumbles to the floor. In the bathroom, he pushes one of many unmarked buttons on the wall, and the shower is turned on, soaking his fully clothed wife. Cut back to the thirty-year-old. No, she'd better find her hapless parents a less futuristic hotel.

The spot fails. What's the target market here? Thirty-year-olds who plan vacations for their parents, or are going to send them on one as an anniversary gift? Not a very big market, I bet.

Does this hotel and vacation website really want to alienate Baby Boomers and older generations?

What bothers me is not the idea that older people would be unable to "figure out" a high-tech hotel room, but that they are portrayed as too ignorant to find a hotel for themselves on the internet, and must rely on their web-savvy children. *This is factually incorrect. Baby Boomers are not only the largest demographic connected to the internet, but are also the largest demographic for web-based product purchases.* We know our way around cyberspace.

Would the spot have worked with a different slant? Probably. Using humor in advertising is often a question of point of view. If a socioeconomic group makes fun of itself, it's often funny and effective. If a socioeconomic group makes fun of another socioeconomic group, you run the risk of alienating a secondary or hidden market.

The spot with the futuristic hotel would've been fine had all the principals been Baby Boomers (or all an older or younger generation). It would've worked had all the principals been in their early thirties, although, as I've mentioned, the "plot" would have been repeated. It doesn't work if the object of ridicule is another generation.

Recap:

Advertising campaigns, and the products and services promoted, often take on lives of their own—appealing to market segments you may never have imagined. As important as your target market is, it's just as important not to alienate secondary and hidden markets when overseeing and critiquing campaigns.

CHAPTER THREE

How Boomers Want You to See Aging

WHEN A FRIEND OF MINE was in his early forties he made an appointment with his doctor. He was in good shape. He exercised regularly, ate well, took care of himself for the most part. But something seemed wrong, off kilter.

He told his doctor that over the last few years something felt somehow different. Many mornings he would wake up with aches; it was difficult to get his day going; he was tired in the early afternoon; had trouble concentrating without taking a breather or two. Sometimes he felt like he needed a short nap.

He'd been playing tennis for twenty years, but lately it was a struggle to get through more than two sets. Add to this a few digestive problems now and then. More than once a week he had trouble sleeping. Of course, that made it even more difficult to sleep because he was worried about what might be wrong with him.

The doctor recommended a complete physical. My friend agreed. A few days after the physical, he went in for his consultation. Obviously, he was apprehensive—having no idea what he was about to be told.

Five minutes later the doctor entered with a clipboard overflowing with computer printouts and reports. After exchanging greetings, the doctor sat down, leafed through the ominous-looking jumble of papers, and said, "I've been looking this over today, earlier in the morning, and just now, and I think I've narrowed down a diagnosis."

"Yes?" my friend said, dry-mouthed.

The doctor looked up, then into my friend's eyes, and said, "You're getting older."

My friend jerked and blinked. "WHAT?"

Then he laughed.

And the doctor laughed.

This seemingly silly anecdote tells us a great deal about how we Baby Boomers see ourselves. It also touches on what we don't see about ourselves. While my friend was baffled for a moment, and his laughter was partially from relief that there wasn't anything seriously wrong, he was really laughing at himself for not grasping the obvious. My guess is that the doctor knew the diagnosis during the first consultation. He'd probably been through scenarios like this before.

There is a similar episode in Gabriel Garcia's novel, *Love in the Time of Cholera*. This is a universal theme.

The Age Question

Barring any serious diseases or accidents, most Baby Boomers will age gracefully. The fact is that we're not always aware that we *are* aging gracefully. Sometimes it comes as a complete surprise that "getting older" is going so well for us.

But who actually thinks about his or her age all the time, or even very often? While there are artificial milestones attached to aging, from birthdays to graduations to anniversaries, only a small percentage of people are obsessed with how old they are. And there will always be a small percentage of people of all generations who worry about their age, who act and dress as if they were twenty-five years younger.

However, all these disconnects do not necessarily mean that you should advertise to people as if they were younger—or older. Advertise to a sixteen-year-old as if he or she were fourteen and you'll be in big trouble. Perhaps advertise to sixteen-year-olds as if they were eighteen, but be careful.

Market to a fifty-two-year-old as if he or she is thirty-two or sixty-two, and you'll create the same cognitive dissonance.

If using models for Baby Boomers in ads, it might be a good idea to shave off a few years. Nobody needs to see *all* their imperfections, or well-earned crow's feet, shouting at them from a page of a magazine or embedded in a television screen. (Images sometimes *do* emit painful or pleasing sounds, by the way.)

When you are targeting any market, age is simply one of many cohorts. But this does not mean that campaigns should mention age. Advertising aimed at Baby Boomers with themes such as "Because you're older" or "Feel (or look) young again" can be jarring to the senses. It may leave a bad taste in many mouths. A consumer may be feeling pretty young at the moment anyway, or be feeling so old that your message might seem like a slap in the face. The subtext may imply a specific age range, but there is rarely a need to point it out. How many children enjoy being told they are children? How many teenagers love being told they are teenagers?

If you are developing a campaign for a toy or game for pre-teens, you will try to convince the target market that it is an exciting, technically savvy product. You don't tell them it is a great game because they are between the ages of seven and twelve.

The same holds true for Baby Boomers. When critiquing an ad campaign aimed at Baby Boomers, make sure the message focuses on the product or service, not on the age the consumer happens to be.

And contrary to social commentators, the media, and certainly advertising agencies—most of the time we are who we are: people in our middle age, not much different, but a little different, than other generations were in their middle ages. We're not jumping in mosh pits juggling cans of soda pop, trying to relive our youths. If we want to do that, we have ample music CD collections or home recording studios. We buy Harley-Davidsons and drive them at safe speeds.

But most of the time we're perfectly happy, or miserable, or just slogging along, being whatever age we happen to be.

However, in other important ways Baby Boomers are actually redefining what middle age is. We are not rebelling but changing, calmly challenging misconceptions about middle age.*

*More about this "age thing" is discussed in chapter twelve.

If you want to make sure this ethos seeps into copy and design, the best bet is to make sure people working on the campaigns are experiencing this same ethos.

CHAPTER FOUR

Give Boomers Room for Choices

THE WAY MOST Baby Boomers plan on designing their futures is another important ethos to consider when fashioning or critiquing campaigns.

> "Baby Boomers think they never will get old," said Myril Axelrod, president of Marketing Directions Associates in New York. "This self-image will have a lot to do with their future housing choices . . . Boomers are not considering retirement housing. Instead, they call it next-stage housing."
>
> —*Chicago Tribune*[1]

The first part of the above quote is a bit tongue-in-cheek. Unfortunately, advertising agencies often interpret this kind of statement as "Baby Boomers want to be eighteen to twenty-five again." This is another misconception—and a common projection. That's because copywriters and creative directors see everything through their own eyes. They think Baby Boomers want to be *their* age. Again, advertising creatives have problems understanding that they are merely doing what comes naturally to them: marketing to themselves.

The second part of the quote, *"Boomers . . . call it next-stage housing"* rings true. If you analyze how Baby Boomers think about what they want in this area, you can learn some valuable lessons and apply them to all products and services aimed at Baby Boomers.

Attracting Baby Boomers to planned communities has become a major headache for developers of housing, retirement communities, and realtors, and ultimately to advertisers. Boomers are now begin-

---

1 Handley, John, "Building for Boomers is Seen as a Growth Market," *Chicago Tribune*, 2004.

ning to scale down, and eventually will semi-retire or retire. What will we want and not want when it comes to a planned community?

Past generations tended to get excited about modern conveniences that would make their lives easier. They would walk into a planned housing unit and exclaim, "Look! It's got this and this and this and this!" The more features, the better. The more "planned," the better. It was time to start a new life. They wanted to be rewarded for all their hard work, and relax.

Not so with Baby Boomers. We take most modern conveniences for granted. We don't want to start new lives, but continue the lives we already have.

Baby Boomers will be anticipating a seamless transition. Instead of "Look! It has this and this and this," we'll be sniffing around for friendly, useful spaces. You will want us to say, "Look! There's a perfect place for my pottery wheel," or "There are plenty of windows and sunlight. My house plants and indoor herb garden will do fine in here," or "Good. I can put up big, deep shelves for my books and CDs," or "Here's the perfect room for our side business on eBay," or "Here's a place where I can soundproof a recording studio or have an entertainment center," or "This oversized back door is great because I can get my bicycle in and out without squeezing and jerking it around, and the extra-wide hallway means there's plenty of room so I can just lean it against the wall and we won't bang into it every time we walk past it." These will be the selling points. For Planned Communities, less is more.

Baby Boomers have also been fodder for the ergonomic revolution. Developers take heed: it had better be easy to get around or you'll lose us. For example, I love to run up and down the stairs. The problem is that I can't run up and down narrow, small stairs anymore. Big, wide, easily negotiable stairs I can handle. I want to keep running, or at least happily skip, without tripping over myself too often.

Taking the Planning Out of Planned Communities

We are also a bit jaded when it comes to advertising. Everything is and will be a tough sell. *With such a huge emotional and financial invest-*

*ment, convincing us that we should soon be lugging our lives into a retire-
ment or semi-retirement community will be the toughest of sells.*

The common term used for such places is "Planned Communities." However, when presenting planned communities to the public,
Baby Boomers could wince at the concept. You know it's planned,
we know it's planned (What else could it be?)—but "planned" may
sound too restrictive to Boomers. We don't like the idea of anything
planned. We want to do it ourselves, construct our own lives. Let us
sustain the illusion, or a partial illusion: communities are not planned.
We do not want to live in prefab theme parks. "Next-Stage Housing" sounds a bit stilted, but at least it's on the right track.

Some Baby Boomer sociology experts predict that semi-retirement
and retirement communities will naturally develop *personalities* based
on shared interests. These could be gardening, motorcycles, vegetari-
anism, the arts, even a community where the shared interest might be
financial speculation.

Brent Green, author of *Marketing to Leading-Edge Baby Boomers,*
believes that many 50-plus communities will become hotbeds for social
activism. If we have a resurgence of our youthful activist days, it may
be to pick up where we left off—revivifying proactive sensibilities
Boomers had as teenagers and young adults, an idealistic fervor that
"once gave us the greatest sense of engagement and meaning."[2]

When developing or molding a community for Baby Boomers,
start with the concept of "neutral." Do not confuse this with "sameness." For example, when designing an indoor community space, do
not assume that it will be used mostly for Bingo. Fashion it with flexibility so that it may be used for almost anything. Think of a hand-
crafts fair, a concert venue, a town meeting, or an internet-ready video
conferencing center. The technical specifications must be able to handle all sorts of activities. Don't think that a couple of electrical outlets, a simple PA system, and a few racks of folding chairs will suffice.

The same holds true for community spaces outdoors. A truly imaginative site designer will be able to envision almost everything in the

2 Brent Green, *Marketing to Leading-Edge Baby Boomers* (Ithaca, NY: Paramount Market
Publishing, Inc., 2005)

spaces available—without designing it for anything in particular. Lawn bowling, shuffleboard, and checkers might not be the activities of choice for Boomers. Again, less is more. The residents will add the "more": community gardening, mini-swap meets, fund-raising picnics, extra space for RV parking—who knows. *Baby Boomers will continue to be a vibrant, creative bunch. Don't try to second-guess us.*

The only required feature you can count on will be easily accessible walking-jogging-bicycle trails. We've become health-conscious, and this won't change. If a community is adjacent to a maintained trail, this may be a determining factor for many potential buyers. Certainly more so than a community gym, for high-quality personal exercise equipment has become easily affordable.

Here's another big issue: rumblings in the community planning industry are confirming their biggest fears—*a large percentage of Baby Boomers will shun retirement communities, opting for mixed communities.* This is less a fear, and more a possible retooling of all non–retirement communities. Should developers and planners build units or houses and facilities for Baby Boomers in some, all, or most planned communities, and advertise them as such? My gut feeling is yes.

This group of Baby Boomers can be broken into two segments: first, the folks who have a fear of retirement and getting old and will avoid the stigma; second, Boomers who truly enjoy and get inspiration and sustenance from living in an eclectic culture. This latter segment could end up being a bigger chunk than most experts are predicting.

Selling Universal Design to Baby Boomers

Universal Design, originally developed for people with disabilities, is a major player in the housing industry.

For many (but not all) Baby Boomers there is still a stigma attached. If not for the disabled, Universal Design (UD) is for *old people*—and Baby Boomers, according to popular myth, eschew anything that smacks of "old" or "senior." UD is patronizing and condescending—as if we're babies again and in need of playpens so we won't hurt ourselves or get into much trouble.

UD is a great blueprint (as a metaphor and in reality) for planned communities, individual units, and any combination thereof. However, a delicate touch is needed when marketing Universal Design to a healthy, vital demographic.

Ergonomics. That's not such a negative word to Baby Boomers. We've been the fodder for the ergonomic revolution. We almost feel as if we invented it. The concept resonates.

But an "ergonomically designed home" sounds rather cheesy. Using the word sparingly in any marketing/advertising collateral is a good idea. For example, *ergonomic* works when describing kitchens, but not bathrooms. Everybody wants a simple-to-maneuver-in kitchen. It makes cooking and entertaining easier. But not too many healthy, active over-fifty folks want to hear about ergonomically designed bathrooms—until they've used one.

The way most Baby Boomers plan on designing their future is an important ethos to consider when selling Universal Design. Whether they know or not, a majority of Boomers would appreciate the benefits of UD. And UD is a perfect example of "less is more" and the idea of a neutral empty space so Boomers can be creative and move their "lives" into a malleable unit.

Aging in Place

I've heard this term defined a few ways. The simplest definition: people staying put in their condos or houses for the rest of their lives. Others refer to "aging in place" as remodeling current residences with Universal Design as the blueprint. Still others use the term to describe Baby Boomers moving into condos or active adult communities not far from where they are now—so they can still be near work, family, and friends.

A presentation I gave in the summer of 2006 in Phoenix at the National Association of Homebuilders' 50+ Housing Summit had a large section dedicated to the "problem" of aging in place. It's a problem, of course, for AACs. How do you convince Baby Boomers to consider your offerings—whether your community is across the country or across town?

The first slide in the aging in place section was titled, "Let's talk about your competition." I tossed up logos from Del Webb, Robson, Meritage, and a few others—along with one of a real estate salesman outside a house with a "for sale" sign on it. I shook my head. "These are not your competitors," I said, "this is." A new slide popped up that read "Home Sweet Home." Most in the audience nodded.

Then I talked about Margit Novack's Moving Solutions,[®]—a company specializing in transporting the parents of Boomers who are in their 70s–90s to assisted care living facilities. Moving Solutions does everything: meets with the mother or father or both, packs everything, unpacks everything, and sets up the new residence so all he/she has to do is walk in the front door.

To Margit's surprise, a big chunk of her business is now Baby Boomers wanting her franchised companies to move *them*: a Moving Solutions representative discusses where everything should go in the new residence, the client take a vacation for a few days—and enters the new house or condo with everything unpacked, put away, and set up.

There is a sociological ethos here. A large percentage of Boomers have been and still are leading non-linear lives, so "starting a new life" doesn't have much meaning to them. According to Matt Thornhill of The Boomer Project, Boomers often reinvent themselves every five years. Continuing your life means continuous change—even if you live in the same place.

As I mentioned earlier in this chapter, when deciding to change location, the ethos of many Baby Boomers is this: Move *my life* over here. It's not: Move *me* to a new life. Again, "less is more."

I've yet to see any AACs grasping this ethos. Marketing and advertising copy needs to be retooled or tweaked. Boomers are a diverse, unwieldy group. No one message speaks to all. My advice to the attendees was to think about this powerful but overlooked ethos and work it into existing marketing materials.

While I wasn't about to create copy out of thin air, I tossed out a handful of marketing ideas. Here were two:

1. Floor Plans seem to be merely an afterthought on most AAC

web sites. I would bump up their visibility. You could produce an interactive, three-dimensional tour of the interior. Include measurement rollovers for every nook and cranny in every room and hallway. Don't forget the garage. Show windows, electrical outlets, and any other features. This will make it easy for mouse-wielding Baby Boomers to virtually fill in the spaces with their "lives." Will this or that fit here? Which room would be best for a bedroom? Which for an office? Will my desk fit under the window? Will our bikes fit in the hallway by the back door, or will we need to keep them in the garage? These web site visitors will become actively involved, asking questions and finding answers. It's impossible to superimpose a life over a skimpy, two-dimensional abstract.

2. In a 2005 Pulte/Del Webb Baby Boomers Study, 64 percent said travel is their top unfulfilled ambition, and 45 percent said that travel will be their #1 expenditure in the future. How can AACs take advantage of this? One of the fastest growing internet business models is the non-linear vacation house swap. This is where someone in Florida offers his/her residence for a month, stays a month in a residence in England—while the owner of the residence in England stays in Italy, etc. Your AAC could partner with one of these businesses, making your offering more attractive to a potential buyer. For example, these extras: easy listings on the house swap site, all amenities included during a swap (golf, swimming pools, workout facilities, etc), a "welcome package" of information and discounts in the local area for the vacationers. Remember this: *what you're really doing is selling this service to the potential home buyer.* It will be easier to swap a residence with someone if living in an Active Adult Community.

What "Less Is More" Really Means to Baby Boomers

"Less means more" means room for choices. Remember this when analyzing campaigns for any product or service.

Baby Boomers do love to read, often chewing on every single word in a brochure or print ad. They want to know *everything* about a product. But when all is said and done, they will sit back and wonder if this product or service will complement their lives and help create more choices. They are not looking for a product to change their lives or give them a quick fix.

Less is more also means more control over the product. A good example of what I mean is included in the next chapter.

CHAPTER FIVE

Boomers Pay Attention Longer

> Early impressions tend to coalesce into a natural view of the world. All later experiences then tend to receive their meaning from this original set.
>
> —Karl Mannheim, Social Scientist 1951[1]

PSYCHOLOGISTS, SOCIOLOGISTS, AND HISTORIANS have all gotten their shots off about the effects of mass media on Baby Boomers during our adolescent years. Let me nudge one into the fusillade: Most Boomers grew up watching television and listening to the radio. There were hundreds of television shows, scores of radio stations, tens of thousands of commercials.

We were the first generation of children to be bombarded with both audio and visual electronic media, but the last *not* to be able to frenetically click away if an image, a voice, a sound, or a sliver of music didn't suck us in immediately. Our spastic fingers were not wrapped cozily around remote controls. (What we did with them, I don't remember. When fidgety, I probably tickled my younger siblings.)

Even for late Baby Boomers, those bulky remotes were slow and clunky. How many channels were there? Five? Seven? Did you even bother with UHF? As a kid, I don't remember ever commandeering the push buttons on the car radio. Just sitting in front was enough of an honor. There was always the risk of back-seat banishment with the babies. I was the perfect gentleman, lording over the rabble in the rear.

---

1 Steve Gillon, *Boomer Nation: The Largest and Richest Generation Ever, and How It Changed America* (New York: Free Press, 2004)

In my room, a transistor radio was next to my bed. I listened to two, maybe three stations, smoothly dialing in each with a twirl of a thumb. But how often did I do this? Once every ten minutes? Every twenty? Mostly, I stayed tuned to the same station until some song came on that I just couldn't stand, or couldn't stand hearing again.

It was the same with television. The difference: a *TV Guide* was always within reach. I knew what was on and watched a show from beginning to end. And that included *all* the commercials.

Commercials were long back then—a minute. They were mini-stories. Flash fiction. I'm not sure if a kid today would even recognize a minute commercial *as* a commercial. He or she would probably think it was a music video, and would wonder what the name of the artist was. (That was who? DJ Headache Anacin?) More likely, they would've clicked away before the product was even mentioned.

Back to Baby Boomers as kids: Compared with our parents, we developed short attention spans. Our lives moved quickly; our media moved quickly; our choices flew by and through us like white tornados. However, when comparing Baby Boomers as kids to what GenXers and Echo Boomers experienced, we were mired in molasses. Add to the mix maturation and, if sucked in, we can follow a base-ball game or hour-long news show from start to finish—*and* sit through most of the seventy-plus ten-second promos and commer-cials. We won't remember many of them. But we'll watch them.

Pouncing Mouses

Many sociologists and futurists are predicting a few more radical social and political upheavals triggered by Baby Boomers before we're packed off in coffins and urns, sprinkled over mystical mountains and mundane golf courses, or blasted into outer space so we can eternally commune with the cosmos.

On the other end of the spectrum, we'll also be revolutionizing the tourist industry for the next thirty years, taking hundreds of millions more vacations before the ultimate holiday. Travel companies are having big problems trying to figure out what to offer—and how to reach us. We're not lining up on docks for meaningless cruises on silly ships, nor are we allowing ourselves to be bundled into cookie-cutter cavalcades so we can gawk at decaying castles from the lumpy seats of double-decker buses. Nobody is going to tell us what a vacation is. We'll tell you.

There's a cottage industry out there preying on the blubbery and frightened tourist industry, making wild guesses as to what Baby Boomers will want to do with all our free time. I won't list them all here. They range from ecologically correct junkets to health-nut boot camps to intellectually and culturally themed excursions to the beating down of well-publicized, well-traveled "unbeaten paths."

This book deals with advertising to Baby Boomers, but I'll overstep my bounds and propose a business model: *Boomers are internet-savvy. Boomers are not passive. We do not want to simply slap one key and have our vacation pop up on a screen.* We want to rattle lots of keys, have our mouses pounce and bite off appetizing chunks of graphic and description from all sorts of sources—and build unique, variegated vacations.

Some smart dot-com entrepreneur will partner with thousands of travel companies, resorts, hotels, museums, airlines, car rental companies, and build a modular travel and reservation website. Myriad tempting experiences will be offered. The website will calculate the price of each activity, cataloguing and coordinating everything. *It will be a package you fill with goodies.*

Planning it will be half the fun, and immediately entice and involve the site visitor. For a few days you'll be lying on a beach. The next day you'll travel to a large city and take in whatever sights you wish, perhaps joining a guided tour. In the morning you'll be driving to a tennis resort for a day or two. After that will come a scenic road trip to a local winery for a prearranged private tour. Keep driving, and you'll check into a secluded lodge, and hike in the mountains for a few days. Then you're off visiting another city in another country, mostly to just goof around. Finally, check in your car, hop on a train, and before long you're naked and slumping into a vat of hot mud at a famous health spa, followed by a shower and reservations at a five-star restaurant.

You could even spend an afternoon in lumpy seats on a double-decker bus if you want.

Possible Copy/Campaigns:

- We don't tell you what a vacation is. You tell us.

- Package your own vacation.

- The unPackaged Packaged Vacation

- Tell us what a vacation is. Then take it.

On the surface all this sounds like "more is more." Not really. It's the same as offering big, empty rooms in planned communities so Baby Boomers can bring their lives with them. It's the same concept as starting with neutral (but not sameness).

Again: Less Is More

It also might seem as if I'm contradicting myself. On one hand I'm saying that Baby Boomers' attention spans have widened and deepened, aren't as frenzied as they once were, and certainly aren't as chaotic as younger generations. On the other hand I'm saying that we're not passive, we like to "rattle lots of keys, have our mouses pounce and bite off appetizing chunks."

It's a balance of choices *and* control that we're after, within the context of neutral spaces—real or virtual. If you have a product or service, *let us imbue it with meaning.* Present the product or service, let us fashion it the way we want. Position your product, but don't make it immutable. If you start telling us *why* we need something, a "we're jaded, we've-seen-it-all" impenetrable B.S. shield goes up. We won't listen.

Just tell us what it is. And you can tell us as much about your product or service as you want; the more the better.

"More Is More" when describing your product. "Less Is More" when you impose your own meaning and relevance on your product.

Which bleeds into the next chapter about (don't cringe) *Infomercials.*

CHAPTER SIX

Why Infomercials May Be the New Boomer Advertising

IT'S THAT UGLY WORD, conjuring up half-hours of tacky, humdrum hucksterism. But it's the content that's clumsy, not the concept. If the advertising industry ever gets the message, mature, imaginative, absorbing infomercials will be an important way to reach Baby Boomers and other demographic groups.

Throughout most of the last century print was king, even during the age of radio and the early years of television. Jingles, slogans, crisp copy—and when television arrived, animation and clever visuals— were still the poor cousins of privileged print.

Beginning in the middle 1960s, dazzling cinema-like spots mixed with the succinct wit of print became the pinnacle of advertising mastery. An effective television campaign often did it all: customer awareness, imprinting, positioning, branding, and messaging.

Not so today, at least for Baby Boomers. And it isn't simply because we're not being targeted. The real reason is that our attention spans are longer. We want to know more. We need to know more for a product or service to be imprinted. A 30-second salvo will miss us by a mile. We will subconsciously (oftentimes consciously) dismiss it.

If television advertising was once the poor cousin to print, nowadays infomercials are the bedraggled outcasts of both. While there are exceptions, infomercials are shoddy also-rans in the advertising world. There is no money for production, no creativity whatsoever. The in-the-studio-with-an-audience infomercials are reminiscent of the locally produced shows of yesteryear. If it's a location shoot, there is likely to be a simpleminded script, a dull host, and a video crew with no creativity or vision. Not surprisingly, you end up with a simple-minded, dull half-hour with no creativity or vision. *Non*-infomercials.

Okay. I admit it. If I see one more hapless, third-rate TV personality walk into a drearily framed shot, hit his or her mark, say something stupid, and walk off-screen, I'm going to kick in my plasma screen.

There have been inklings. Already, some ad agencies and their clients are taking advantage of the internet and Cable TV, including the "on-demand" format for infomercials. Procter & Gamble has a series of infomercials targeting young men: a "reality show" to promote Old Spice Red Zone body wash. Even TiVo has "created its own platform of longer-form ads with sponsors like cruise line Royal Caribbean Cruises Ltd. and financial services company Charles Schwab Corp." [1]

For targeting Baby Boomers, this longer form opens up possibilities and techniques not normally applied to thirty-second or one-minute commercials.

Here are a few ways of approaching production:

The cliché "thinking outside the box" applies here, but with a twist: think outside the *television* box. The first TV commercials were simply radio ads with announcers onscreen holding up products. Soon, images replaced the mundane, and commercials became more like print ads; they told stories with copy and visuals. Some were mini-dramas, mini-comedies. They also were severely storyboarded. Half of the reason they were storyboarded was to initially pitch the client.

In the Sixties, many commercials became more free-form. A concept based on a slogan or jingle for a commercial was pitched, and creatives had (more or less) free reign to shoot and edit. For example, Wells, Rich & Greene's revolutionary spot for Alka-Seltzer, "No Matter What Shape Your Stomach Is In, " was a montage of close-up, quick-cut vignettes of stomachs. No doubt it was storyboarded, but I'll bet the final edit deviated from the original storyboard cells.

Baby Boomers are perfectly at home with a freer form of art, of

---

1 "Procter & Gamble Makes On-Demand Ad," Reuters News Service, 2004.

entertainment. Many movies from the Sixties and Seventies were scripted but loose, with plenty of room for improvisation by the actors, the director, and the cinematographer. Movies were more "real." Even some television shows (*I Spy, Mash*) at least gave the illusion of improvisation. Rock musicians improvised onstage more than they do now. Our comedy was off-the-cuff, or appeared to be (*Robin Williams, Saturday Night Live*).

Storyboards and Boomers

Special-effects movies must be storyboarded (or at least large chunks of them). Cartoons *are* storyboards. However, if you are targeting Baby Boomers, and you storyboard an infomercial (especially by committee), it will end up DOA.

Products and services are real, and you want to convince potential customers to use them in real life. Anything over-staged and lacking authenticity will seem fake. You don't want your product or service to be perceived as simply a prop or backdrop.

With a short commercial, there isn't time to do much of anything but pitch the product—simply, cleverly, memorably. If there is a whiff of authenticity, your ad agency has gone beyond the call of duty, or you were lucky.

But with the long-form infomercial, a genuine relationship between your product or service and target market is vital, and you have plenty of time to develop one. If it's non-stop pitch, pitch, pitch—you'll lose them.

> Another way to improve campaigns, said Larry Light, executive vice president and global chief marketing officer of the Mc-Donald's Corporation, is to consider agencies "as creative resources" rather than corporate entities that assign accounts to specific employees at specific offices. "That's the future, not to assume the office you've been assigned to has all the creative geniuses you need."
>
> —Stuart Elliot, *The New York Times*[2]

---

2 Elliot, Stuart, "Consumer Advice for Advertisers," *The New York Times*, October 11, 2004.

Finding the Production Talent

The longer-form infomercial has little in common with 15- and 30-second commercials. Different techniques should be used; a different aesthetic should predominate.

Infomercials targeting Baby Boomers (and probably for all demographics) also have little in common with television entertainment shows. They really should be thought of as short films: part cinema, part documentary. Also remember that more and more people are buying large screen TVs and home entertainment systems. Why give them a TV show when you can offer them a mini–motion picture?

There is a form known as *documercials:*

> Often produced in the standard 28 minute, 30-second package for a 30-minute broadcast slot, documercials are one part of a growing industry trend that has blurred the lines between the commercial and the news documentary. The subject matter may not include blatant hard sells for kitchen gadgets or feature a huckster spraying black goop on his bald spot, but documercials are still used to sell a product . . .
>
> —Greg Barr[3]

Start with the above concept, and expand on it. Add a cinema aesthetic. I'd call these *cinemercials*, except that a few companies already use this term for the short commercials made specifically for movie theatres.

If you approach your advertising agency with the idea of an infomercial for Baby Boomers, here are a few things you should consider: Of course, Baby Boomer creatives should produce, as well as write and direct. Finding these creatives within an agency will be difficult, probably impossible. Even an agency's list of freelance producers, writers, and directors won't include many, if any, Baby Boomers.

There are a dozen (maybe two dozen) wonderful, accomplished Baby Boomer film writer/directors, editors, and cinematographers who haven't directed a film in ages. Some are now producers. Some

---

3 Barr, Greg, "Documercials Mean Big Business," © AVVMMP-Access Intelligence, Inc.

work in television. Some produce or direct commercials, or both. Some have perpetual projects in development. Some are sitting around doing nothing.

I'll mention no names, because who knows if the above paragraph might offend some of them. It shouldn't, for I admire many of these folks. They are out there, and may or may not welcome being approached for a well-produced, high-quality infomercial. (The problem, again, is *that word*. Documercial is better, but still doesn't quite define the concept. How I wish I could call them *Cinemercials!*)

Medium-to-small advertisers and agencies can successfully apply the principles above. However, there are pitfalls. Because of relatively inexpensive video cameras and computer editing software, there are thousands and thousands of professional video companies. The good news is that more true talent has developed in this area. The bad news is that there are many, many film and video companies that advertise themselves as professionals but really have no idea what they're doing, and never will. I can use a video camera. I can edit. I do neither professionally. However, I have produced, directed, and written award-winning marketing, advertising and promotional videos.

A cliché worth revisiting: Surround yourself with talented people and they'll make you look better.

I live in the Seattle area. There are hundreds of professional film and video people and companies here. There aren't as many as in New York, Los Angeles, or Chicago, but enough to make it difficult to track down the best talent.

After using a few companies and freelance camera and video people, I stumbled upon one whose work stood out. Why? This gentleman had gone to college and majored in still photography. By chance he ended up with a video camera in his hands and worked for many years in the news department of a local television station. What a combination. Nobody even comes close to this fellow when it comes to lighting and composing a shot.* What a find. I twice took him to Italy for shoots, and Rick Steves would be envious of the footage.[4]

* He's Jeff Erwin of Digital Production Services in Seattle.

---

4 Rick Steves has written many travel guides, and has a popular travel series on PBS.

I also went through numerous editors. One was recommended to me. I called her, we chatted.

I said, "I don't do much storyboarding."

She replied, "What's a storyboard?"*

I knew I'd found one of the best editors in The Great Northwest.

* Of course she knew what a storyboard was. She'd edited many videos for Microsoft.

Infomercials Need Infusions of Money, Talent, Vision

At some point in the Sixties, someone convinced somebody that one-minute commercials could be exciting, absorbing, mini-masterpieces, *and* do their jobs. If you're interested in reaching Baby Boomers, now is the time to persuade agencies and clients that this is likewise true for five-to-thirty minute infomercials.

CHAPTER SEVEN

Internet Advertising for Baby Boomers

THERE'S REALLY NOT MUCH OUT THERE in the way of internet advertising except in the obvious industries like health, travel, and retirement communities. Even *they* aren't doing it right, according to Dick Stroud, a 50-plus marketing authority in London.

His book titled *The 50-Plus Market: Why the Future Is Age Neutral When It Comes to Marketing and Branding Strategies* (Kogan Page), has been written in conjunction with OMD (*www.omd.com*), one of the world's biggest media buying agencies, which conducted a global research program into the way age does or does not affect consumer behavior.

The 50 Plus Market covers much of the world, with research and numbers-crunching from Europe, Australia, Asia, and the United States. Even if you're not marketing globally, your particular region will stand out in bas-relief, giving you a unique and valuable perspective.

And Dick has one of my favorite marketing blogs. The old codger (oops . . . I mean the *age neutral* codger) consistently whips up interesting quips about the 50-plus market (*www.50plus.blogspot.com*).

"Most older web users prefer using 'goal-centered' navigation," Dick told me. "This is a fancy way of saying that the navigation should anticipate the user's questions and provide a simple way for them to get answers.

"For instance, if you think your website user might have difficulty in selecting the most suitable product, then *provide the information to aid in making the decision*, and clearly label it (example: *Which Product May Be Right For You?*). All too often the navigation reflects the structure and priorities of the company rather than taking into consideration its potential customers."

We talked a bit about well-produced, non-hype infomercials, and if Baby Boomers would actually make the effort and sit through them on the web or on television.

"Internet advertising is the fastest growing type of advertising," he said. "This means a lot more than just banner ads. Increasingly it means large format interactive ads, search-engine marketing (optimization and key-words), creating special promo videos for web download, supporting TV ads with online sites, and so forth.

"But to answer your question, 'Yes.' Baby Boomers will sit and watch five, ten, or twenty minute advertising videos, but with two big caveats: the videos have to be relevant, and they must be given the choice to watch them or not.

"Where sites make a *massive* mistake is when they do not give the user the option, or present enough information so they may make the decision of whether to exchange ten minutes of their lives to watch a web video or some other type of download.

"I know it is a much overworked and hackneyed phrase, but it is *all about customer choice* and giving them the information to make a decision."

The problem, we agreed, was that there is usually too much garbage to wade through.

"Let me give you an example of an industry that has not understood this simple point," Dick continued. "It's the Cruise Industry. They persist in using rich media (mainly Flash) on their home page. Yes, you have the SKIP object somewhere on the page, but a lot of people have no idea what that is or what it does. Many are forced to watch some tacky Flash sequence."

And they get tired of this really fast. Most of the time, it's an immediate turn-off for Baby Boomers. *Give them the meaty options right up front.* A simple click for pictures? Videos? A quick link to copy about the cruises? It's all they need. You've lost them if they first have to suffer through meaningless images and empty copy slithering and skidding every which way.

Flash intros are not like intros (title segments) for marketing or advertising videos. Flash intros are usually pointless, have little to do with (for example) a specific cruise or vacation, and are perceived as pure hype and a waste of time. Flash presentations are vacuous branding vehicles, a technique that makes most Baby Boomers queasy and irritable

"My research shows that older people are fine with the 'advertising stuff' on the web" Dick said. "As long as they feel that they are getting the information they are seeking."

Dick often runs into a brick wall whenever he tries to educate businesses about many of these subjects. "50+ advertising using conventional channels is getting a great deal of give-and-take discussion nowadays, but very, very few people are even thinking of asking the same questions about interactive channels.

"What interests me is the style and format of online advertising. In my view it is even more youth-centric than print or TV. There is still this daft idea that online equals youth, and *only* youth."

Breaking Through The Blandness

AN ARTICLE IN *The Wall Street Journal* details "a growing number of new ventures targeting aging baby baby boomers . . . and their $2 trillion in annual spending power."[1] Add to this a bevy of projects not mentioned that I know about—each with hefty venture capital. Be prepared for an onslaught of commercial Baby Boomer web sites, magazines, and even radio and television projects premiering over the next six months.

The problem? Almost all the web sites have the same bland, pandering, motivational messages and graphics.

A sampling of current Baby Boomer-targeted branding messages, mission statements, and corporate tags (or, as we used to call them, *slogans*) include:

Redefining Life After Fifty!

You've had one "prime of life." Now, as an active Boomer, you're ready for your "Second Prime!"

Don't Just Live Longer. Live Bigger. After 50 Life Becomes Yours.

Our mission is to inform and inspire the Boomers and to promote a new vision of life after fifty.

Our mission is to encourage our readers to live bigger. To take risks and pursue their dreams.

Our vision . . . is to rewrite the rules of getting older and transform the voice of aging from one of limitation to one of possibility.

———— is a media company focused on empowering individuals to live the lives they imagine.

---

1 "Still Sexy at 60?," Kelly Greene, Wall Street Journal, July 25th, 2006

If you absorb most of the marketing fodder, along with the scores of recent newspaper and magazine articles about Baby Boomers, it's obvious that the members of this unwieldy, diverse generation are having no problems redefining what it means to be the ages they are. For better or for worse, it's a big part of what they've been doing for the last four and a half decades, and they won't be stopping anytime soon. No motivation required.

I seriously doubt that these pointless messages have done much resonating. And even if they have, enough is enough. If everywhere Baby Boomers click they see inspirational/aspirational branding silliness, eyes will begin to glaze over. (When *you* read through the collection above, you got a little sleepy, didn't you? Or perhaps irritated?)

Three years ago I stumbled upon England's Millennium ad agency web site (in England). I gulped and bucked. Images of people over fifty on an advertising agency web site! Never had I seen this. Quite revolutionary, quite exciting.

And it caught on. However, as with most original concepts, the imitations tended to be watered-down versions of the original. At first it was refreshing to see folks over forty-five portrayed in ads and on the web—but now almost every 50+ site is centered around generic photos of smiling, vapid, mindless people in their fifties and sixties, usually in warmup suits, always prancing around beaches, if not staring lovingly at one another. Enough is enough.then in groups, arms draped and tucked every which way like groping octopi.

Enough Is Enough

If successful web sites and advertising of any sort are to be created for Baby Boomers, there needs to be another revolution. Advertisers and marketers are getting wise to the Baby Boomer opportunity—but I don't see any real revolution brewing in the advertising industry. There are dozens of campaigns, only a few inspired. Most seem to be merely *about* inspiration.

While it will be hard work (as it always is), we have one advantage: instead of cutting through the clutter, we simply have to break through the blandness. ▧

CHAPTER EIGHT

Viagrafication or What Drugs
Really Mean for Boomers

PFIZER AND ITS marketing and advertising agencies don't need *my* help figuring out how to promote Viagra™ to Baby Boomers, or to any other demographic. The word *viagra* isn't merely a brand anymore. In various slapdash forms it's now a noun, an adjective, a verb, a modifier, and, if you think about it, it's practically become a conjunction. It certainly *conjoins*.

But what about the newer "Viagraish" drugs on the market? How do they differentiate themselves and establish brand identities? You'd have to be on Prozac, meaning, "or Zoloft, or Wellbutrin, or Paxil" to think that you can take on the established lexicon. They'll probably try. And fail.

The irony is that they don't have to try. The best thing they can do is simply go with the overflow.

A brand name becoming ubiquitous, becoming part of our mimetic culture, can be both good and bad for the original product's brand perception. If I say to someone who has a headache, "Take an aspirin," I'm really advising that he or she should take *something*, and the person knows this. It can be whatever their preference is—Tylenol, ibuprofen, or if they have a prescription, something stronger.

Many doctors, after deciding a patient might benefit from a serotonin uptake inhibitor, will describe these medicines as "Prozacian" or "like Prozac." Is this good for the brand Prozac? Maybe or maybe not. Ubiquity often dilutes. To many, the fuzzy perception is that Prozac is not a brand name but a group of anti-depressant or anxiety pills. This ambiguity benefits all the other products.

Whereas it's vital to differentiate your product, it's just as important to associate yourself with the established and proven brand name (read, group of products). This doesn't necessarily mean that you should mention the brand name in your campaign, but alluding to it, even giving it a subtle positive spin, will reflect favorably on your offering.

The folks at Pfizer will yell and scream "Me, too-ism!" and "Copycat products!" Let them scream. "Me, too-ism" is a derogatory concept that is talked about among advertising and marketing professionals. It's not something the public is interested in.

Levitra (GlaxoSmithKline and Bayer) will benefit most by emphasizing an association with Viagra. Apparently, the drugs work the same way, although the side effects are different. Levitra's ads have been lambasted by a few in the industry for alluding to recreational use.

Well, golly gee. I hate to inform everybody, but the cat's out of the bag. While it's difficult to tell whether the brand name Viagra has been helped or hurt by all the wacky e-mail spamming going on of late, I dare Pfizer (or any of the other companies) to fashion a commercial warning people that their product is not for recreational use or there will be dire medical consequences.

Many young to not-quite-old-yet males, for various medical reasons, have erectile dysfunction. Viagra and the other drugs may very well be the difference between having sex or not. But other than that, what *is* Viagra for if not recreational use? Unless you're a porn star, I can't imagine taking it before going to work.

Viagra has probably saved a lot of marriages, and that's the point. Marriages and relationships are part hard work, part responsibility, part fun and recreation, and part romance. If Viagraish drugs are taken to alleviate the hard work or responsibility parts of a relationship, I'm afraid you've got bigger problems than erectile dysfunction.

I've had perhaps a bit too much fun with the last two paragraphs, but remember: "recreation" is one of many reasons for taking allergy and arthritis medications, having elective hip or knee replacement surgery, or even agreeing to a regimen of serotonin reuptake inhibitors. We all want to improve the quality of our lives.

Cialis (Icos Corp. & Eli Lilly) will have the most problems getting its complex message across to the public. Cialis stays potent for up to 36 hours. It has been touted in Europe as "The Weekend Viagra." Sounds like fun at first, but what does this mean? Will you be tripping over yourself like some priapic Egyptian statue come alive? Do you really want to be "high" for almost two days? The Cialis campaign accents "spontaneity" as one of its selling points. But what exactly is spontaneity? Is it a random libidinous thought as you walk down the street? Eyeing a pretty girl sitting in a restaurant?

There will be many situations where the perception will be this: a drug with a shorter duration is preferable. But even if you like the idea of a "viagra vacation," does this mean that you'll need two prescriptions, one for Viagra or Levitra and one for Cialis? Can you take Viagra one day and three days later take Cialis? Will your bottle of Cialis be put way in back of the bathroom cabinet and be brought out only for special occasions? Will you ask your doctor for only three or four pills in your prescription, because a full bottle might expire? Will you forget about them?

These are knotty questions. There are answers, but synthesizing and simplifying a single, clear message will not be easy, even when initially marketing to General Practitioners and Urologists. You know how they just *love* to take the time to explain things to their patients.

Creating Silly Scenarios

There is plenty of marketing fodder available about Viagra and the other drugs; plenty of fodder about their advertising campaigns and their effectiveness. However, let me propose one of those "throw the numbers out" types of campaigns.

While it's more complicated than this, essentially these drugs improve the blood flow to certain parts of your body. In fact, Viagra was originally developed to help angina patients. Making this clear in advertisements would not be lying, or even stretching the truth. What a perfect, succinct, direct message.

Yet what we see are men throwing footballs through rubber tires, couples all of a sudden being "in love again" and acting silly, bathtubs overlooking sunsets, and vague, meaningless statements by celebrities.

"Silly" translates into "insulting." This is *not* how consumers (certainly not Baby Boomers) enjoy being portrayed. I've yet to meet anybody who hasn't smirked at the ads they've seen about Viagra, Levitra, or Cialis. It's the *Geritol Syndrome* I discussed in the introduction of this book:

> You can amuse, but don't assume. Give us the facts. Pitching to the emotions instead of the brain is the biggest mistake agencies make when marketing and advertising to Baby Boomers.

Again, this is because 99 percent of the people creating and producing these campaigns are not Baby Boomers. If they were, emotive advertising to Baby Boomers might be effective, and not offensive.

People take prescription drugs for all sorts of reasons. There is nothing particularly embarrassing about high cholesterol, high blood pressure, or other age-related afflictions and conditions. I doubt that someone would say to themselves, "Gee, the doctor wants to prescribe a drug for my high cholesterol. If I take it, I'm somehow admitting to myself that I'm *old* and can't eat the same foods as younger people. And heaven forbid someone finds out that I'm taking drugs to lower my cholesterol! I'd be so embarrassed! I don't want anybody to know my body isn't the same as it was when I was twenty!"

Two or three times a week I take my bicycle out for a spin. There is a nice, flat trail near my house. Every so often I play golf. Not often enough I mow the lawn, and perform various other non-fun physical chores. I usually take some ibuprofen before doing these activities. It lessens the aches a bit. I feel better. Should I be *embarrassed* about this? I don't remember having (or wanting) to take mild pain relievers before or after physical activity when I was in my twenties or thirties.

Ad campaigns for Viagra and the others make you think that simple truths are embarrassing. Instead, they come up with demeaning scenarios that obfuscate the true nature and benefits of the products. They think that Baby Boomers will be embarrassed or take offense at ads that might talk about physical limitations. What they don't know is that we take offense at ads that make us look like we yearn to be macho again, or portray us as batty, inane piles of human mush falling all over ourselves.

Unless you have the serious condition of erectile dysfunction, taking Viagraish drugs will not invigorate your sex life. You will not fall in love all over again. They're not like taking steroids. Yet they are advertised as if they were *legal* steroids, or self-medicating aphrodisiacs, or as if you were swallowing arrows shot by Cupid.

Not only is all this nonsense, but what these advertising agencies are ignoring is this: The truth is *even better.*

Personal Experience

I had a physical not too long ago. Among the many questions the doctor asked was "And how's your sex life?"

"Fine. No complaints," I said.

As I was driving home, I realized that I wasn't paying attention. The question had been an open invitation for a prescription of you-know-what.

While I told the truth, I probably should've elaborated: "Well, considering I'm fifty-three, sex is just fine and wonderful and emotionally and physically fulfilling. True, maybe I don't do it quite as often. It's not quite as edgy as when I was in my twenties. I don't get quite as "whatever" exactly like I did many years ago. A weekend of sex is doable, but can be hard work, and not only for me. Everything seems to work fine. I guess the way to put it is that overall, considering my age, it's just as good, in some ways better than ever, but everything isn't quite as peppy as before. Overall, I imagine my sex life is like most people my age. Why do you ask?" And the doctor would have started scribbling.

Feel free to call the cops after reading the next sentence.

I "procured" a couple of these pills from a friend. After a bit of research on the web to make sure taking one wasn't going to kill me, I took one.

What's to report?

Things worked better.

Obviously, there was a bit more blood circulating through certain unmentionable parts of my body. It was very pleasurable. My more-significant-than-I-am other enjoyed herself, too.

Was it like the difference between night and day? No.

Did we fall in love all over again? Not any more than if I had bought her flowers unexpectedly, or remembered to butter her toast evenly all the way to the edges and not leave it as a sloppily-spread lump in the middle as I usually do.

Am I really macho again? Or *finally* macho for the first time in my life? Hey, I can lob footballs through tires as well as any twenty-year-old, with or *without* a Viagraish drug sloshing through my system. (But a couple of ibuprofen might even the playing field.)

These drugs simply improve the blood flow to certain parts of your body. Is this so embarrassing? Do you really have to create silly scenarios?

Want to break away from the pack?

Just tell the truth. In a thirty-second ad, or better still, in a trenchant, no-nonsense infomercial.* After the facts are out in the open, future campaigns can feel free to incorporate a bit of tongue-in-cheek fun. Why not?

* Oddly enough, on Pfizer's website there is a simple explanation of how Viagra works. If the ad producers just used this as the script, they'd leave the competition in the dust.

The good news for these companies is that most Baby Boomers are not afraid of drugs, *or* sex. If our "liberation" needs to be lubricated by rolling a tablet into our gas tank to get that old engine purring again, so be it. No big deal.

And you can use these techniques and principles for almost any drug when fashioning campaigns for Baby Boomers.

CHAPTER NINE

Get Rid of the Stereotypes

THERE'S THIS BIG ORGANIZATION out there. It caters to older people. I won't mention the name because I'm about to say some not-so-nice things about it—and who knows—the powers-that-be might get offended and hire some retired, grizzled gangsters to visit me and break my artificial knees with their ergonomically-correct canes.

Among other activities and services, the organization publishes a handful of magazines (actually, *one* magazine with different versions for specific age groups, sort of like *The Weekly Reader* when we were kids).

The younger "kids" in this scenario are Baby Boomers, and we're not lining up in droves to join the organization. To make matters worse, advertisers and marketers aren't lining up to target us, so the kinder-garten version of the magazine is not attracting sufficient advertising revenue.*

* They'll dispute this, but the percentage of Baby Boomers joining compared to older generations is scaring them. While not a direct corollary, the B2B ad campaign targeting media planners and advertisers is part of their plan to boost Baby Boomer enrollment.

To solve this, the organization decided to advertise to advertisers, and hired an advertising agency to do this. The organization and the advertising agency want marketing and media planners to know how wonderful and numerous Boomers are and how much discretionary income Baby Boomers have so they won't ignore us anymore.

Now comes the fun, exciting part: the advertising campaign has one ad with ashen-faced Baby Boomers in body bags ("These days, doctors don't pronounce you dead. Marketers do."). Another shows Baby Boomers acting like testosteroned teenagers ("Outta the way, punks: older racers are the hot-rod kings!"). Yet another has one of a middle-aged lady dead in a powder room (probably from overdoing it on the dance floor) with police chalk outlining her body. I don't know what the copy is because I haven't seen it. It's probably something like, *"Give me wrinkle cream, or give me death!"*

The problem is that the advertising agency, like most agencies, is very much caught up in the trendy concept of *Branding* (one of those buzzwords overused in the last few years, and often misunderstood), and consciously or subconsciously did a bit of branding with their client's product.

They've done this by introducing and presenting the product as immature, daft, and half-dead. Quite the product I'd want to buy (meaning: quite the demographic I'd get all hot and bothered about advertising to).

Even if this campaign convinces advertisers and media planners to consider targeting Baby Boomers, these silly stereotypes have been reinforced and will be carried over into consumer campaigns.

Personally, I'm not offended by all this. In my free time I write all sorts of caustic fiction and columns, and more often than not make fun of myself and Baby Boomers in general. To be honest, I wish *I* had thought of the idea of two people in body bags chattering away when I was penning pretentious, avant-garde plays thirty years ago.

But this is business, folks. If you were trying to promote teenagers as a marketable group for a product or service, you wouldn't show them with erupting volcanoes of acne, blankly staring at mindless video games. If your job were to encourage a client to consider the 65-plus market, you wouldn't portray them nodding off, half-falling out of chairs, drool running down their chins. *You would present these demographic groups as alert, desirable, and potentially interested in your product.*

Baby Boomers have been branded. We're an unwieldy, varied, complex social group. We've lived through interesting times. We're living through interesting times again. Cultural, political and economic upheavals—along with getting older slowly but (we're hoping) surely —keep us on our toes, relentlessly challenging and rearranging our interests and priorities. In order to reach us, the advertising and marketing industry must *un-brand* Baby Boomers, whether you're selling us or selling *to* us.

Do not assume that you know who or what Baby Boomers are. You'll get it wrong. And if marketers and advertisers continue to "brand" us, we'll run you over in our hot rods, toss you in body bags, and dance the Hully Gully up an' down an' around an' around your chalk outlines.

Even More Irony, More Mixed Messages

That big organization, the one that gave its stamp of approval for branding Baby Boomers as immature, daft, and half-dead, oddly enough *has stringent policies when accepting advertisements for its magazines*: No negative stereotyping of older people. No crackpot medical devices that would give the impression that older adults are physically or mentally incapacitated. All advertisements should have an optimistic spin. Getting older is a positive experience, not a negative one.

While I think they could loosen up a bit (the ads in their magazines are rather antiseptic), as a whole, this isn't a bad philosophy when accepting advertising targeting Baby Boomers. But here's my question: Would this organization accept its advertising agency's ads promoting the 50-plus market (placed mostly in media or marketing trade publications) in *its own* magazines?

Undoing the Damage

Although you've heard a lot of complaining from me so far, quite honestly I don't think there has been much damage. I'll tell you why soon, but first let's assess the damage: What should we consider damage? Damage to what? To whom?

- Advertisers have damaged themselves by ignoring Baby Boomers. This can be reversed.
- Advertising agencies have damaged themselves. This can be reversed.
- Baby Boomers have *not* been damaged.

True, outside of the advertising and marketing world Baby Boomers have become punching bags of late, especially in the media. Brent

Green writes forcefully and eloquently about this in his book, *Marketing to Leading-Edge Baby Boomers*.[1] All his points are valid. However, Baby Boomers *themselves* haven't been damaged much. A few bruises, maybe some scratches.

We're a resilient bunch, having spent most of our lives altering the status quo, questioning authority. We're not that thin-skinned, and for the most part feel pretty good about our lives, our accomplishments. Sure, we have some regrets. Who doesn't? But we will continue to make positive contributions to society for the next thirty years.[2]

Yes, advertisers have ignored us. We've been branded. Maybe we scratch our heads and wonder why. Perhaps we feel a bit disenfranchised.

However, we're still buying products, still avid consumers. We're just forced to waste time figuring out which specific products or services would be best for us because marketers, advertisers, and ad agencies are not giving us any information. The information we *do* receive isn't directed at us, usually isn't to our liking, often degrades us, and generally gives us the heebie-jeebies. We turn away and ignore it. As I explained in chapter one, this hardly qualifies Baby Boomers as victims.

However, if you as an advertiser want to consider yourself a victim, fine. A better idea might be to concentrate on your future, not your past. With diligence, you can expand your customer base by focusing a healthy chunk of your advertising resources on this vibrant, very much alive demographic.

---

1 *Brent Green, Marketing to Leading-Edge Baby Boomers* (Ithaca, NY: Paramount Market Publishing, Inc., 2005)

2 I recommend reading *Boomer Nation: The Largest and Richest Generation Ever, and How It Changed America,* by Steve Gillon (Free Press, 2004) and *Age Power: How the 21st Century Will be Ruled by the New Old* by Ken Dychtwald (Jeremy R. Tarcher, 2000).

Don't Paint too Rosy a Picture

AN ARTICLE IN *USA Today* asks us to "take a moment to journey forward to 2046, when 79 million baby boomers will be 82 to 100 years old."[1] A paragraph later, the reporter asks, "So just what kind of America will be forged by this crowd of geriatric goliaths?"

Excuse me for being an unassuming "David" (or even worse, a genocidal Grim Reaper) but I doubt very much that *all* 79 million Baby Boomers in the U.S. will still be alive in forty years, swaggering like giants, unless the medical establishment is holding out on me.

The good news you know. Many Baby Boomers will live longer, healthier lives—more so than in any previous generations. The bad news you also know. By 2046 a huge chunk of Boomers will have passed on, and another huge chunk will be dealing with acute diseases and afflictions.

The problem is that well-meaning articles in the press like the *USA Today* piece, along with mountains of 50+ marketing fodder, are setting up Boomers for a psychological fall. There *will* be a backlash.

I'm not a psychologist, but common sense tells me that if it were beaten into my head repeatedly that things are going to be just peachy for the next forty years, that my same-aged friends will all be around laughing and cavorting while leading meaningful, vigorous lives and then, shock of shocks, many of us become incapacitated and/or drop and die, I would feel cheated. I would become depressed and disillusioned. It will happen even if I'm one of the lucky healthy ones.

Ask today's 80+-year-olds about this or that and you'll probably find that many are surprised (but relatively pleased) they're still alive. They believe they've beaten the odds, for whatever reasons. Jump twenty-five, thirty years: if the myth of the non-dying, perfectly healthy Baby Boomer persists, folks in the aging industry are going

---

1 "2046: A Boomer Odyssey," Marco R. della Cava, USA TODAY, October 27, 2005

to have millions of very angry octogenarians their hands. They might even blame you for all those false promises.

How should marketers and advertisers deal with this? Contrary to popular myth, Baby Boomers do not believe that they are still teenagers or young adults. (Some do, but they need therapy.). Boomers are slyly redefining what it means to be the ages they are. Included in this new definition are some youthful attitudes, but the real change is that instead of winding down, many are winding *up*. We're not looking forward to retirement, we're looking forward to new lives, new challenges. Only a small percentage will opt for pure retirement.

This is all part of redefining what it means to be the ages we are. It may seem to some as pathological, believing and acting as if we're eighteen or twenty-five—but that's because pundits and experts suspiciously eyeing this gargantuan, spirited, unwieldy, and varied hoard of middle-agers have nothing with which to compare it. The only conclusion they can come to: Baby Boomers must be a bit daft.

There is a big difference between thinking you are younger than you are, and not thinking that you are old. This "night and day" distinction may confuse many pundits, but it does not confuse most Boomers.

Much of this new, positive attitude about our future has to do with being the beneficiaries of so many fast and furious medical advances. Some we have already taken advantage of, while others are ready and waiting for us, some just—or right around the corner. A good example is joint and hip replacement surgery. The cane industry is in the doldrums, and we're hoping it will never recover. (Actually, the cane industry has been replaced by the walking stick industry, which promotes more aggressive trekking. Just another way Baby Boomers are changing the norms.)

Another medical advance is pain management. This promises Baby Boomers and successive generations freedom from a fear that haunts us all as we age.

There has been plenty of press about Baby Boomers and their dread of Alzheimer's. Not much of a surprise. Alzheimer's affects many of our parents, we're caring for them, and nothing frightens us more than not being in control of our own destinies. However, from what I've read there may be some breakthroughs within the next twenty years. That's very good news.

Am I painting too rosy a picture here? Isn't this something I was railing about in the first few paragraphs? Yes, but with a big difference. All the examples above have to do with the *quality* of life, not the *quantity*.

If I were digging into a marketing or advertising campaign for a client in the aging industry, I would focus as much as possible on the high quality inherent in the product or service—and toss out any (or most) mention of longevity. This would hold true even with basic nutritional and exercise products. A significant chunk of people who eat only healthy foods and exercise regularly die of heart attacks, get cancer, are the victims of all sorts of diseases and afflictions. You can't fool me.

But the *quality* of their lives of those people who live healthy lives in every respect will be superior to the ones who don't take care of themselves, or avail themselves of what's out there in the aging industry market.

Nobody can promise you that you'll live to be a hundred. However, you can (more or less) make a good argument that healthy lifestyles and advances in modern medicine will offer you a quality life after sixty that no preceding generation had even imagined.

I'm fifty-five. I may die in five, ten, twenty, forty, or fifty years. If you promise Baby Boomers longevity, I will know at some point that you are not telling me the truth. However, if you promise me a certain amount of *quality of life* if I take advantage of medical advances, lead a healthy lifestyle, and buy and use your products and services, I'll probably believe you.

And I'll continue to take your word for it until my dying day.

The next section of this book will help you find a top-notch advertising agency (or do the advertising yourself), communicate effectively with your agency, critique campaigns, and much more. ▪

PART II

Finding the Best Marketing and/or Advertising Agency

CHAPTER TEN

The Best Advertising Creatives Advertise to Themselves

> Amongst democratic nations, each new generation is a new people.
>
> —Alexis de Tocqueville[1]

THERE HAVE BEEN some great writers through the years, creative folks who have been able to grasp the psychology and ethos of humans of any age, in any age. William Shakespeare, Charles Dickens, Leo Tolstoy, William Faulkner, and Gabriel García Márquez are a few who come to mind.

And there have always been a handful of people around who can sell ice to Eskimos. The chances of finding one or the other, or better still, a combination of both, are slim, so you have to play the odds.

Over the last one hundred years or so, the best literary writers have been the ones who have written about their own generations. We all have our favorites.

This doesn't mean that there haven't been exceptions. There have been. The same holds true for advertising creatives.

But why take chances with your product or company? If you can find a commercial illustrator, photographer, graphic artist or copywriter who can reach all generations, who can sell walking sticks to twenty-year-olds and skateboards to octogenarians, hire him. (And if I could find a lady advertising creative with one of these talents I'd *marry* her, and stop doing this stuff for a living. Extended European vacations, community volunteering, and local golf courses beckon.)

---

1 Alexis de Tocqueville, *Democracy in America,* Chapter XIII: Literary Characteristics of Democratic Ages.

Play the odds.

Unfortunately, the deck is stacked against you at most advertising agencies. As I've explained in previous chapters, nine times out of ten they don't have any seasoned, Baby Boomer creatives employed (anymore), so of course they'll try to sell you what's in stock, even if it isn't the style you want and doesn't quite fit. They'll gently dissuade you from harboring such silly notions as demanding creatives who are part of the same generation as your target market. Some of the big agencies might even *pompously* dissuade you.

A Personal Story

When I started doing research on the Baby Boomers market, not much was being said about advertising. Mostly it was all about marketing, the numbers, the failure of media and companies to target Baby Boomers, and why they should (again) take this market very seriously.

After I had a good idea of what I thought about all this, and a few well-received advertising-to-baby-boomers articles were under my belt, I happened to get a call from a local agency in the Seattle area, where I live. They wanted to meet me after reviewing my resume. Someone there had stumbled upon it online.

As yet, my CV said nothing about Baby Boomers. It was full of other fun, impressive stuff, but for all they knew I was twenty-five, dressed in black, had eleven tattoos, and hung out at raves with my Blackberry. (As if I were any different when *I* was twenty-five, what with my flowered shirts, striped bellbottoms, and bulky, tooled-leather shoulder bag stuffed with bean sprouts and record albums.)

I thought this was the perfect opportunity to give my spiel, my "pitch" about advertising to Baby Boomers, why and how this should be done, and to make it clear that I would appreciate being considered for any campaign where the client wanted to reach this ample demographic.

I'm pretty good at pitching. That day, you would have thought I was pitching leprosy as a cure for acne. I have to use a couple of clichés here because this is exactly what happened: *Their eyes glazed over. They thought I was nuts.*

"We don't have many clients who want to advertise to Baby Boomers," one person said. The others nodded with relief.

He was lying. The agency has *no* clients who want to advertise to Baby Boomers, because if a client did, everybody at the agency would talk him or her out of it.

I dropped the whole thing. I bombed. Had I kept going, no doubt they would have called security, and ushered me out to the street. An ambulance and straightjacket would be waiting for me.

I might as well have walked into the room and said, "Consider me when you have clients who want to advertise to extraterrestrials." And I would've heard, with the same straight face, "We don't have many clients who want to advertise to extraterrestrials."

"But there are 76 million extraterrestrials. They spend $1 trillion annually on goods and services, have more than $300 billion in discretionary income. They also control . . ."

And here comes the security guard.

Their eyes glazed over. *But mine opened.*

Nobody will be convincing ad agencies to target Baby Boomers except clients and potential clients. That's because if you demand that they do, and *demand that they hire the right people for the job*, well, that's a lot of money they won't receive if they don't land your account.

Now let me tell you how they'll try to talk you out of targeting Baby Boomers.

CHAPTER ELEVEN

Excuses Ad Agencies Use to
Self-Fulfill Their Prophecies

I'VE SPRINKLED many "excuses" for ignoring Baby Boomers throughout this book, but here are a few more. These are among my favorites when ad agencies deign to consider Baby Boomers:

We reach them anyhow. They watch TV and see the commercials, buy magazines and see the ads. And they have to buy products anyway.

Sure we do.

Here's an example of the way Madison Avenue wants you to think: For years, pre-teens and young teenagers never paid any attention to toothpaste ads. But for the last decade or so, toothpaste has been developed, manufactured, and marketed to kids and teenagers. Forty-odd years ago toothpaste was marketed to adults only. Crest began targeting parents, claiming fewer cavities for kids with Crest, implying smaller dentist bills.

Did we, as children, care? Not really.*

However, if you watch toothpaste ads today, you would think that people brush their teeth up until their early thirties and then all of sudden they magically turn seventy and buy only denture cream. (I guess in Madison Avenue's alternative universe, this is why all senior citizens lose their teeth. They haven't brushed in forty years.)

* Now teenagers care — maybe not about cavities—but certainly about blindingly-white teeth. *And* they get fewer cavities. A good trade-off for parents.

So what brands of toothpaste *do* Baby Boomers use? According to ad agencies, the same ones we used as children, because . . .

Baby Boomers don't change brands.

Of course we don't, at least in Madison Avenue's out-of-touch alternative universe.

For example, I'm wearing the same style shirt I wore almost forty years ago. The Nehru collar is fraying, and while it isn't as stiff as it once was, at least it doesn't dig into my double chin. I haven't bought a car in just as long because . . . well . . . I just can't find another Corvair. And my hair is a tad unkempt around the edges because my corner drugstore doesn't carry Brylcream anymore. And, since I won't change brands, there's no way I'm switching to Vitalis.

One trillion dollars annually on goods and services.
Three hundred billion in discretionary income.

But I won't switch to Vitalis. Won't even try it.

Let's get back to toothpaste. And let's pretend that you are a tooth-paste manufacturer or marketer: Contrary to what you may believe, most people over forty brush their teeth.

Are you twenty-five? Do you use the *same brand of toothpaste* as you did when you were seventeen? Do you even remember what brand you used when you were seventeen? If you're thirty-three, do you use the same brand of toothpaste you did when you were twenty?

At the moment, in my bathroom, I have a tube of something called *Aquafresh.* I'm not sure why I bought it. Maybe it was on sale. Maybe the phrase "Extra Fresh" or "Triple Protection" caught my eye. Maybe I had no clue what might be a good toothpaste for me at my age. They're all probably as good or as bad or as harmless as toothpastes are for your teeth. What do I know?

When I was a kid, I brushed with *Colgate.* I didn't buy it; it just showed up in the bathroom. I can't pinpoint when I actually changed brands for the first time, but as I sit here, wistfully reflecting on my life, it seems to me that I've used many different brands of toothpaste. I remember *Gleem,* something called *Pearl Drops,* something that was red (or at least the tube or box was red, it's all a haze now) that had a very strong, icy-hot flavor. Definitely woke me up. And *Tom's of Maine.* And *Rembrandt.* I remember buying at least one tube of Rembrandt because it was such an odd name for a toothpaste. Not many sparkling, toothy smiles in those otherwise glorious portraits by the Great Dutch Master.

So what toothpaste should I buy? Anybody have any ideas? I have a trillion dollars in the bank, and 300 billion to spend as I please. And I'm sauntering around the dental care aisle, hands in my pockets, jingling a few million in loose change, looking up and down, side to side, and I'm not sure *what* I'm going to buy.

As advertising agencies have told you, I'm going to *buy something*. I guess it doesn't matter to you whether I buy *your* product or not, because *I'll buy something . . .*

Here's an alternative universe you might consider. And it wouldn't be such a bad one for me, either:

"Hmmm. What's *this* toothpaste? I think I've heard about it. Saw a commercial, read an ad about it. The person in the ad was around my age. She talked a bit about dental care, a bit about gums, about teeth, how to keep them healthy and strong. She had a nice smile, but not one that blinded me, sending me stumbling, feeling my way to the bathroom for the Visine. And the box doesn't look like it's an ornament for a science fiction Christmas tree. Maybe I'll buy it."

Back to *Baby Boomers don't change brands*: This is silliness. We've changed brands for years; we continue to experiment as consumers, and we'll keep experimenting for the next quarter century.

No matter what age you are, there are probably two or three consumer brands you won't change. I imagine it would be pretty difficult to get me to try a new ketchup; maybe mayonnaise, too. Not that I buy cases of these items. However, they're comfort condiments. I like seeing them around.

Other than that, I'm wide open for suggestions. Pitch me. If you don't, I'll buy whatever I want. No one is trying to persuade me to buy *your* product, that's for sure.

But let's say I'm wrong—or even partially wrong, and that marketers and advertisers are correct. Baby Boomers *don't* change brands.

Why would we change brands when we're not being targeted? If no one is trying to sell us soap, we'll just buy the soap we normally buy. What is pulling us to *your* product?

Nothing.

By telling you that Baby Boomers don't change brands, advertising agencies are really promoting a skewed, self-fulfilling prophecy: *If Baby Boomers don't change brands, it's because nobody is giving them compelling reasons to do so.*

Pitch us. If you don't, we'll buy whatever we want.

Or keep selling to everybody else. We'll sort of watch commercials out of the corners of our eyes because they have nothing to do with us. We'll flip through magazines, not stopping to read the ads because they're not speaking to us. We'll poke around on the internet paying scant attention to the advertising bells and whistles. Then we'll meander around stores, making up our own minds, probably sticking with brands we know, or, for no particular reason, giving this or that one a try.

Let me repeat a quote that is at the beginning of this book. It's by one of the giants of advertising, from an interview in the early 1960s. Lop off a few years from the age he mentions, think a bit about the complex marketing done now but not done then, and ask yourself if it applies today:

> No, I don't think a 68-year-old copywriter can write with the kids. That he's as creative. That he's as fresh. But he may be a better surgeon. His ad may not be quite as fresh and glowing as the Madison Avenue fraternity would like to see it be, and yet he might write an ad that will produce five times the sales. And that's the name of the game, isn't it?
>
> —Rosser Reeves[1]

Remember what advertising agencies have told you: Baby Boomers buy products anyway. Don't demand that your advertising agency hire the right people to create campaigns to target us. If you do that, your company might increase sales by 25 to 50 percent.

I've said two or three times that you should play the odds.

What I'm really saying is this: Play it safe.

---

1   Denis Higgins, *The Art of Writing Advertising* (New York: McGraw-Hill, 2003).

CHAPTER TWELVE

One More Feeble Ad Agency Excuse

THIS AGENCY EXCUSE is possibly the most convoluted and egregious of them all.

"Baby Boomers have never grown up. They have created and sustained the illusion that they are much younger than they are. So when you target 19-to-35-year-olds, you likewise reach Baby Boomers because they think they are still in their teens and twenties."

This is a complicated one to discredit because there are kernels of truth in it. However, its twisted, one-dimensional conclusion is *so far off the mark that this advertising philosophy will alienate Baby Boomers.*

Some Simple Psychology

Most people don't like getting old—at least physically old. If you're lucky enough to be spared debilitating diseases, you'll certainly be affected by any number of afflictions. A small percentage of people pathologically reject their chronological age. These folks have been a part of every generation.*

* Trying to look younger with Botox, hair transplants, and other cosmetic solutions is often economically beneficial, perhaps even a necessity. There is age discrimination in the work force. The largest number of complaints filed with the EEOC is now age discrimination-related, replacing race and gender discrimination.

For the rest of us, it's basic human nature to think of yourself as a bit younger than you are. This is because we have no "forward" age perspective to draw on, only "backward" age perspective.

As I write this, I'm fifty-six. But I really don't know what being fifty-six is. I *do* know what being in my middle forties was. I remember being in my middle forties. I have age perspective on both sides, so I can isolate that age. At the time I didn't know what being in my middle forties was, how it felt, what it meant. I can't really get my mind around being fifty-six because I don't have a dual perspective. When I'm sixty, I'll know what being "fifty-six" is.

This is true no matter what age you are. If you're reading this and you are twenty-five, my guess is that you have no idea what being twenty-five is. Without a doubt, you remember what it was like being twenty-one. When you're thirty, you'll know what "being twenty-five" was.

So sure, I think I'm a bit younger than I am. I probably "think" I'm in my late forties. But I don't think I'm in my thirties. And if I started to believe I was in my twenties, or still a teenager, I hope a friend or family member would drag me to a psychiatrist, especially before I started thinking I was in nursery school.

People don't walk around thinking about how old they are. I don't leave the house being fifty-six. Nor do I walk around feeling my age.

Actually, I'm a bit of a "Dorian Gray" personality when it comes to age. I've been told more than once that I look younger than I am. I usually answer with, "Yes, but if you see me naked I look about one-hundred and two—so it evens out." As far as feeling younger, it's about the same. Sometimes I feel eighteen, other times eighty-six. Rarely do I feel my age, whatever that feels like. I don't know.

I'm not sure I want to feel my age. I like the variety.

For the next twenty years, Baby Boomers will be redefining what middle age is. Part of this will be a rejection of "getting old" in favor of youthful, vibrant lifestyles. Much of this is due to medical advances. We're healthier. We can replace joints. If heart arteries clog up, operations are now routine—and relatively safe. We enjoy being active, and this will keep us in relatively good condition, mentally and physically.

The noted gerontologist and author Ken Dychtwald believes that old age might not begin until you are in your eighties.[1] Today, the WWII and Silent Generations are doing a great job redefining what old age is.

But remember this: *Right now, Baby Boomers are redefining what it*

---

1 Ken Dychtwald, *Age Power: How the 21st Century Will be Ruled by the New Old* (Jeremy R. Tarcher, 2000).

means to be mature adults in middle age. We are not redefining what it means to be teenagers, young adults, thirty-somethings. We did that already. GenXers, GenYers, and Echo Boomers are doing just fine redefining what these ages mean to them. And advertising by and for them reflects their ethos and speaks to them, as it should.

Baby Boomers do not want to be twenty again, or thirty again. They want to feel as good as they possibly can for the ages they are. They do not want to be marketed and advertised to as if they were young adults or thirty-somethings.

In fact, Baby Boom women are the *real* age revolutionaries. Many are feeling very empowered, very alive, and ready to take on the world. While they could do without some of the wrinkles and some of the aches, ask most women over forty if they would like to live their twenties and thirties all over again, and they'll say, "No thanks. I'm happier and more productive now than I have ever been."

So if an advertising agency tells you "when you target 19-to-35-year-olds, you likewise reach Baby Boomers," they are sadly out of touch with one of the largest, and certainly the richest, market segments today, and you should seriously consider interviewing other agencies.

CHAPTER THIRTEEN

Do You Really Need an Advertising Agency?

HAVE I SAID ANYTHING NICE about advertising agencies yet?

Over the last hundred years, no industry has had more gut impact on American culture than the advertising industry. Advertising campaigns are the patron saints of magazines, radio, television, and now the internet.

Whether anything "nice" was said about advertising in the above paragraph is for you to decide. Nice or not, those are the facts.

I was a Madison Avenue baby. My maternal grandfather was one of the advertising greats of the 1920s through the 1950s, penning an advertising how-to titled "The Simple Simon Stories" (one of the first *Dummy* books). It is still recommended reading in advertising and marketing courses at colleges and universities. My mother was a copywriter. My father was a VP at a major ad agency in the 1950s and 1960s.

I've seen the pretty stuff and the not so pretty stuff, from the inside and the outside. The good, the bad, and the *"Get me a better graphic designer."* I've known and worked with some of the most creative, hardworking and honorable people in the world, and have suffered the sordid shenanigans of common hucksters.

But the answer the question posed in the headline of this chapter, is "Yes." If you are a small to medium-sized business and have a product or service for B2B or B2C, you probably need an advertising agency.

The good far outweighs the bad. I could go on for fifty pages listing the good and the bad, but let me simply turn my appraisal upside down and inside out, and get to the meat of it.

Here's a quote from one of the giants of advertising, William Bernbach (Doyle Dane Bernbach):

A great ad campaign will make a bad product fail faster. It will
get more people to know it's bad.[1]

Imagine what a great campaign will do for a *good* product.

So What's a Great Campaign?

Nowadays, it's hard to say. I'm not even sure what a campaign *is* anymore. There are branding campaigns, viral campaigns, transformational
marketing campaigns, a whole list of odd techniques and theories.

For Baby Boomers, a great campaign should begin by returning
to the basics. We respond to simple, direct messages. And facts.

Do you want to present these simple and direct messages in
entertaining ways? Fine. But don't think that we can be beaten over
the head with branding bats, or taken in by plain-clothed marketers
pretending to be our new friends, selflessly offering us lip gloss and
breath mints.

Viral Marketing

While I have some ethical issues with viral marketing, I won't
impose my values on younger generations and younger advertising
professionals. Viral marketing is hot right now. It may work with teens
and twenty-somethings. If it does, great. Viral marketing may end up
a powerful marketing and advertising technique, or whither away.

However, viral marketing won't work with Baby Boomers. We see
a shill coming a mile away. Don't waste your money.

Branding

About seven or eight years ago I started hearing the term branding being bandied about. It was *the* buzzword, and I wasn't sure why.
Branding Agencies started to pop up all over the place. I scratched
my head. What's a branding agency? I couldn't figure it out.

I finally did: *Branding agencies are advertising agencies that brand them-*

---

1   Denis Higgins, *The Art of Writing Advertising* (New York: McGraw-Hill, 2003).

selves as branding agencies. That's all there is to it. Why they want to present themselves as one-note ad agencies is beyond me. Branding has been an integral part of advertising for over a century. I do have to admit that whoever started "branding" branding has been quite successful at it. (My guess is that it was disseminated using some sort of shady, unethical viral marketing technique . . .)

Here's my advice: If all you want to do is "brand" your product, find a branding agency. If you want to advertise your product, find an advertising agency that knows how to do it all: marketing, campaign creation, copywriting, graphic design, television and radio production, internet advertising, *and* branding.

A Bit of The Good

Again, aimed at the small to medium-sized business, the entrepreneur, the not-so-sure:

Ad agencies are packed with intelligent, motivated, talented, creative business people. These folks are probably not much different than you, and the companies are probably not much different than yours.

Advertising execs may appear to be more flamboyant, maybe slicker than the average businessperson, but in some ways this is merely glossy packaging. They are as interested in nuts and bolts business as you are. Don't let their appearances fool you.

The real story is that business people are as inspired and creative as advertising people. What can be more creative than inventing or designing new products or services, and constantly improving them? And advertising people are as sober, practical, and down-to-earth as business people.

Sure, I've met and worked with some staid, unassuming advertising people, as well as working with a few flamboyant clients, so take what I've said with a grain of salt. These are generalizations.

Dirty Little Secret

That quote from Bill Bernbach ("A great ad campaign will make a bad product fail faster.") cuts both ways. If you have a product or service that isn't up to snuff, isn't going to catch on, wouldn't you like

to know this as soon as possible?* A product
lollygagging in your warehouse or on store
shelves costs you time and money.

Of course, you won't find an account exec
who will say to you, "Let's put together a really
good campaign and get it out the door ASAP
so we can find out if this product is DOA."

* This is assuming that
you haven't done any
market testing (possibly
because you couldn't
afford it, or it wouldn't
be applicable with your
product/service).

But if you think about it, you *do* want to know if a product is
viable as soon as possible. If you have a small company and limited
resources, the sooner you find out the better. A quick death is less
expensive than a long, drawn out one. Large companies may let a
product linger, and eventually write it off. Not you.

Sometimes, advertising is the magic bullet that kills a product,
which in the long run is to your benefit. You can move on to the
next idea, the next product, the next challenge.

A Bit of The Bad

Have I mentioned that ad agencies are ignoring Baby Boomers, and
attempting to convince you to do the same? If you're looking for
more damning fare, you won't find it here. (Although I find the above
blunder quite damning.)

The worst thing I can say about advertising agencies is that they
are very expensive. If you're a small company and don't have the
money to hire an agency, you *can* do some or all advertising yourself
by hiring freelancers, although this may only create headaches, not
good advertising campaigns.

I talk about finding (Baby Boomer) freelancers in a later chapter.

Bottom Line: The good outweighs the bad. Find an advertising
agency.

CHAPTER FOURTEEN

The Search for the Perfect Advertising Agency

I DON'T WANT to talk too much about major ad agencies.* Most that have been absorbed by mega-corporations, have little flexibility, and are set in their ways.

* In the beginning chapters I used some major campaigns as examples. I simply wanted to make my points using print ads and commercials that might be familiar to you.

Major advertisers may mull over some of my suggestions, but as far as insisting on Baby Boomer creatives, I have my doubts that this book will have much impact, at least not at first.

We have another solid twenty-five years of Baby Boomer advertising to consider, so eventually the ad industry (probably from the bottom up) will catch on.

Small to medium-sized ad agencies are where the Baby Boomer advertising revolution will happen. Here are a few reasons why:

- Smaller agencies are more flexible and open to new ideas, new ways of doing things, and creative ways of approaching problems.

- It is not uncommon for smaller and medium-sized agencies to hire freelancers when needed. This is not the normal procedure at big agencies, where many (often too many) creatives are on payroll. If a client suggests or insists on a Baby Boomer creative, a smaller agency won't flinch. They will be happy to insure that the best freelancers are attached to the account.

- Many advertising agencies, large and small, have Baby Boomer owners, CEOs, presidents, VPs, or other executives.

However, with a small or medium-sized agency you can bet that the head honcho is still deeply involved with the creative side. If you make it clear that you want to target the 50-plus market, and you insist on one or more Baby Boomer creatives working on the account, you'll probably end up with the owner or president personally taking over the campaign, or certainly becoming more involved than he or she normally would. This will be to your benefit.

The Best Fit

Assuming that you are a small-to-medium-sized advertiser, a small-to-medium-sized agency will usually be the best fit for you, no matter what your target market(s) might be.

The hierarchical nature of large agencies also bleeds into the creative department. There are "A" clients, "B" clients, "C" clients and so on. There are "A" creatives, "B" creatives, "C" creatives, and so on. If you are a "B" or "C" client, creatives assigned to you won't be from the "A" list.

Under normal circumstances, this is not necessarily a bad thing. If you are a "C" client, it is only because you are a small advertiser, possibly with a new product or service. You don't have the money or the reputation to be categorized as "A" or "B." However, "C" creatives might very well be brilliant youngsters, with talent oozing out of their pores, offering fresh ideas and novel approaches.

Perhaps I've just described *your* new product or service. And who knows? That "C" creative might end up making you an "A" client. Then, of course, he or she will become an "A" creative.

However, if you are advertising to Baby Boomers, there are two pitfalls:

1. You don't want barely twenty-somethings working on your account (at least not in primary positions). You want Baby Boomers.

2. If "C" creatives are older, they may be on their way down.

Bottom Line: The best fit for products and services targeting Baby Boomers will usually be a small-to-medium-sized agency.

Defending Those Big Guys

As if they need defending—especially by me. After all, how did they get so big in the first place? Large agencies have boundless resources, are partnered with PR firms, marketing agencies, media services, and all sorts of juicy ancillary companies.

I have a business friend who was a VP for over a decade at a major PR firm. This PR firm was part of a multinational conglomerate which included ad agencies, marketing agencies, and so forth. Recently, he joined an independent PR firm. The other day he e-mailed me and asked if I had some specific research that might be useful to a project he was spearheading.

I didn't say it, but was thinking, "If he were still working at the other firm, he wouldn't be asking me for this information. He'd be leaning on the three or four advertising and marketing agencies under that ubiquitous umbrella. In fact, I might have been asking *him* for this information had I needed it."

While good ad copy and design are not created by committees but by individuals, brainstorming sessions in the beginning and fine-tuning afterwards often make for great campaigns. Large agencies have at their disposal many creatives (and others) who can contribute.

What's a Medium-sized Agency?

I think of medium-sized agencies as independent. However, many excellent mid-sized agencies have been gobbled up by the conglomerates. Not necessarily a bad thing.

Chiat/Day was once a small agency. Then it became mid-sized. Now it's part of the Omnicom Group. Call Chiat/Day a mid-sized company if you want. Or call it a multi-national. For a long time, Deutsch, Inc. was a smallish agency. Then it became mid-sized. Now it's part of Interpublic Group.*

Both these agencies have been influential and success-ful. Both came of age while advertising to Baby Boomers. (You'll have to ask them what their take is nowadays when it comes to targeting the 40-plus market.)

* And Donny Deutsch, of course, is a brilliant and notorious Baby Boomer.

Depending on the agency and the conglomerate, a non-independent, medium-sized agency may be the best of both worlds. But you might not need all the noise (and cost) that comes with a conglomerate. You might simply require an agency with pure focus and more personalized service, one that can kick-start a modest but effective 45-plus advertising campaign.

So don't rule out independent agencies, small or medium-sized.

As you read on . . .

This book is written for a wide swath of business people, including Baby Boomer entrepreneurs, and entrepreneurs targeting Baby Boomers with their products/services. Baby Boomers are now the largest demographic of new entrepreneurs. There are also numerous entrepreneurs of all ages who are inventing, creating, and manufacturing products and services specifically for the 45-plus market. Many of these people may not be familiar with the advertising and marketing industry. (See chapter sixteen) If you are in the advertising and marketing world, remember that not everybody knows as much about this industry as you do.

CHAPTER FIFTEEN

Interviewing Advertising Agencies

IN MOST CASES, small-to-medium-sized advertising agencies want you as a client. Some good reasons why they may not accept you:

- If a conflict of interest exists, (an account with a product or service similar to yours) an ethical agency will not handle you. However, because they are small or mid-sized, the chance of this is slim.

- In good times, some smaller agencies overextend themselves. Rarely do they turn away business, but it does happen.

- Some agencies do not like to handle products they believe to be harmful. A few might not handle liquor, wine, or beer. Others are environmentally conscious.

- Agencies often turn down political campaigns for (you guessed it) political reasons, or because they do not want to alienate their clients. (If you were a Republican, would you be thrilled about your agency handling a Democratic campaign? And vice-versa.)

- More often than not, small to mid-sized agency owners are very involved with their clients. Some only want to handle a manageable number of accounts. Give them credit for honesty and integrity.

- A few agencies think of themselves as specialists. For example, some agencies specialize in the health industry. They may handle a few non-health, but related products and services (for example, insurance). But if you walk in with a revolutionary new egg beater or a reversible, edible necktie, they might just tell you, "We don't really know much about this type of product, don't know how to advertise and brand it, so you would be better off with another agency." Again, give them credit for honesty and integrity.

Two queasy reasons why they may not want you for a client:

- An agency might consider your company or product or service unworthy to be in their stable. Every industry has snooty companies.

- Related to the above (and practically everything else in this book), they may not want to handle a specific target market because they believe it will reflect poorly on their agency. Along with Baby Boomers and their elders, some agencies do not want to target ethnic groups, religious groups, or certain economic groups.

Of course, this lack of interest is to your advantage. Move on. You *want* an agency that will get excited about your product or service.

The Interviewing Process

If you own a business, you know what to look for when interviewing prospective employees. You know how to evaluate possible business partners. You're discriminating when picking and choosing ancillary businesses or manufacturers that will be working for you. Beyond the usual due diligence, here are some thoughts, strategies, and guidelines when considering an advertising agency:

They're probably not as crazy as they look, or they're crazier than they look. In the advertising industry, some of the most astute business professionals dress with maverick flair, and some of the most talented creatives dress like bankers. I could spew psychobabble about the reasons for this, but I'll leave that to the afternoon talk shows. Just remember: in the advertising business, it's difficult to judge appearances.

An agency's office ambiance will tell you something about how they operate, and if they are flexible enough to accept new ideas (in this case, perhaps the "new" idea of advertising to Baby Boomers). How the office looks and feels when you walk in usually reflects an agency's advertising philosophy. Straight-laced agencies are often rigid in their approaches. More than likely they employ tried and true methods and techniques. These work well for their clients, usually conservative companies with products and services like insurance, pharmaceuticals, and so forth. More creatively crafted offices are generally open to new approaches and ideas. But how open to new ideas will they be? Open enough to hire Baby Boomers? This would produce a potent mix of creatives.

If you have ever been a creative director, or have worked as a director in a collaborative field like theater, movies, or television, you know that it is much more difficult to crank up a creative than to tone one down. If a copywriter is overwriting, a graphic designer's work is too busy, or an actor is chewing scenery, asking for "less" is easier than trying to squeeze "more" out of them. There is always *less* there, but not always *more*. This is why I recommend creative, high-energy companies when considering advertising agencies for targeting Baby Boomers.

More of the Problem, The Conundrum

Actually, conservative agencies would probably be more willing to hire Baby Boomers. That's because more creative agencies are packed with twenty-somethings, who demand that their advertising to be more youth-centric (who taught them that, anyway?), and don't want to deal with the *Geritol Syndrome*.

While I've called this a "problem," it isn't. As I've already stated, the way to reach the Baby Boomer demographic is by *employing Baby Boomer creatives in all advertising agencies* , and by targeting Baby Boomers (even as a secondary or tertiary market) for most products and services, not just the obvious ones. So I'm being a bit argumentative (and possibly wrong) when I say that Baby Boomer creatives might not thrive in more conservative agencies.

Despite everything I've said, I'm convinced that the best campaigns—the *breakthrough* campaigns—will come out of agencies where creativity bounces off walls.

The business community wants remarkable advertising, but turns a cold shoulder to the kind of people who can produce it. That is why most advertisements are so infernally dull ...our business needs massive transfusions of talent. And talent, I believe, is most likely to be found among nonconformists, dissenters, and rebels.

—David Ogilvy[1]

A fact-based campaign crammed with creative elements, with Baby Boomers deeply involved, would be the best of all possible worlds. Conservative campaigns with little or no creative DNA will be DOA.

I have a business friend who wants to start an advertising agency that would only accept clients whose products are for the 50-plus market, and he wants to hire *only* people over fifty, from the receptionist on up. It's hard not to applaud such an idea, but I wouldn't want to work there. And it wouldn't be because of the receptionist. I've met some gorgeous, very smart ones who've mentioned to me that they're grandmothers. (They've *got* to be lying.) The reason I wouldn't work there is because I love working with people in their twenties. They sizzle. They're galvanized. They charge *me* up.

If you want to get on the bad side of an agency immediately, tell them: "My product is for adults, but I would like to primarily target the 45-plus market. Do you have anybody over forty-five working here? Any copywriters? Creative directors? Graphic designers?"

And if you really want to make them your enemy, tell them: "My product is for the 45-plus market, and I'm going to require that one or two creatives, maybe even my account executive, be in that age group. They would be more sympathetic to my product, understand it better, know how to sell it better, and grasp the ethos of that age group."

Or don't say any of the above. Then they will become your best friends. And chances are that you will sell about half the products you probably could.

---

1 David Ogilvy, *Confessions of an Advertising Man* (New York: Ballantine Books, 1971).

CHAPTER SIXTEEN

How to Find Baby Boomer Creatives

I ESTIMATE that there are 3,530 Baby Boom creatives out there somewhere. Here's how I came to that number: Estimates say 76 million Baby Boomers are alive and mostly well in the United States. I figure that 76,000 of them have a flair for writing, illustrating, graphic art, film or video producing or directing, music composing, and so forth. Within this group, I bet 7,600 know something about the power of persuasion, and would excel in the advertising industry. Out of that number, 1,760 of them already have (and are long gone), while another 1,760 or so would probably be very interested in giving it a whirl.

That's quite a cauldron of creativity. If I were an advertiser, I'd hand my ad agency the biggest ladle I could find.

Who Are They?

In the first chapter I talked a bit about this. The vast majority of Baby Boomer advertising creatives have moved on (of their own doing, or not). Can any of them be convinced to return to the fold?

My guess is yes. Many would probably be thrilled. However:

- Most are happy where they are.
- A few might laugh in your face.
- Many would make the sign of the cross and back away.
- Others would hang garlic around their necks and proceed with caution.

The advertising industry can be ruthless, exasperating, and wacky. Some people who've gone in other directions don't miss this. Others thrived on it, and if offered a second chance, might take it.

The Late Bloomer Boomers

> I don't think that you should become a copywriter until you've done something else first . . . I wrote my first ad when I was 39 . . . I couldn't have done it unless I had done a lot of other things first . . . I had experience that was enormously important when I sat down to write my first ad.
>
> —David Ogilvy[1]

One of the ways Baby Boomers are redefining middle age is by beginning new lives. This is nothing that hasn't been done before, but for a large chunk of a generation to do it practically *en masse* took many prognosticators by surprise.

When Baby Boomers were in their late teens through their early thirties there was an explosion of creative productivity in all fields. Now Boomers in their late forties and fifties, the ones who didn't quite "make it" or took safer paths, are finding out that their creative juices never dried up. Many of these folks are writing fiction and non-fiction, becoming graphic artists and photographers, and playing and composing music. And just as many are doing astonishingly creative things in the business world, often as entrepreneurs.

This isn't like retired people taking on hobbies. The Late Bloomer Boomer Movement is going full blast, and there's no stopping it. The magic equation: Thirty-odd years of experience *plus* not feeling old and being relatively healthy *plus* knowing you have another quarter-century of productivity in you equals . . .

Well, we'll see. Some pundits are predicting that Late Bloomer Boomers may leave a bigger imprint on society than the "early bloomer" Boomers who were at the top of their games twenty-five to thirty-five years ago.

Where Are They?

Advertising agencies know where the former Baby Boomer creatives are. They may squirm when questioned. Even the smallest agencies

---

1 Denis Higgins, The Art of Writing Advertising (New York: McGraw-Hill, 2003).

have some clue how to contact people in their cities and communities who once worked in advertising. The Late Bloomer Boomers might be harder to track down because they have no idea anybody might be looking for them. In their new lives, few would even consider advertising, for they know how youth-centric the industry is.

Do you read local newspapers? If so, you might find some interesting journalists who are aged fifty and older. That's because the largest age group among newspaper readers, national and local, is Baby Boomers. Publishers know their markets, even if advertising agencies don't.

I wouldn't want to give you the impression that anybody can just sit down and be a good copywriter, but many successful ones were originally journalists. Fundamental copywriting rules are the same for journalists: Good headline, tell the story in the first sentence or paragraph, and then weave the facts into a narrative. Columnists with a point of view and a spark of creativity are even better. Yes, I'm getting very "basic" here. Some might say simple-minded and pedestrian. But my point is this: From journalist to copywriter is not the biggest of leaps.

From fiction writer to copywriter is also not a tricky jump. You might find some very good local and not-so-local writers of fiction and non-fiction on the internet, what with everybody tacking up home pages and blogs. It's easy to search for resumes and find writing samples. Just go online.

All this holds true for illustrators and graphic artists as well. Many are becoming very successful, or at the very least are finally being appreciated, thanks to the World Wide Web.

If you don't have the time (and have the money) call up an employment agency. Tell them you're looking for someone in their forties or fifties who might not be an experienced copywriter but is a professional writer. What will the employment agency do? Jump online.

While I have a tough time imagining ad agencies, large or small, rummaging around the internet for talent (Baby Boomer or not), as an advertiser with a product for the 50-plus market it might be a good move to find a copywriter yourself, if only to have in your hip pocket when you approach an agency.* "I will supply the copywriter, since you don't have one over fifty, and you do all the rest." My guess is that they will "all of a sudden" unearth a few, and you will end up with more choices.

* Again, this holds true for graphic artists.

Recap:

As a company with a product or service for Baby Boomers, protect your investment. When working with an ad agency to find the best people for your campaign, be proactive.

CHAPTER SEVENTEEN

Should You Do-It-Yourself?

IF YOU'RE A SMALL ENTERPRISE with limited capital, it's possible to put together a reasonably professional website, brochure, print ad, or simply some "copy and pictures" that promote your company or product. In earlier chapters I advised against this. Advertising agencies know what they're doing.

Agencies are not only experts in conceptualizing and producing campaigns, but they work with the best ancillary outfits in the marketing and advertising industry, international, national, regional and local. They have a line on the most appropriate marketing professionals for your product/service.*

If it's really a question of saving a few thousand dollars (or even ten thousand depending on your financial plan), bite the bullet and spend the money. When you see the finished product, that bullet will melt in your mouth like warm chocolate.

* Some would say that I have this backwards. Marketing firms have a line on the best (or most appropriate) advertising agencies. My take is this: if you have modest funds and have developed a small, specialized product, ad campaigns come first. (Marketing agencies won't be happy with me giving you this advice. That's why I'm putting it here in small print. Maybe they won't see it.)

Years ago someone said that under-spending in advertising is like buying a ticket halfway to Europe. You've spent your money but you never get there.

—Morris Hite [1]

You're Not Listening, and Will Go It Alone

One of the reasons for this chapter is the many thousands of new Baby Boomer entrepreneurs. It's not a trend. It's a movement, one that will continue for the next twenty years.

---

1 Morris Hite, *Adman: Morris Hite's Methods for Winning the Ad Game* (Dallas, TX: E-Heart Press, 1988).

While not all Baby Boomer entrepreneurs are developing products specifically for Boomers, many are. Add to this the thousands of non-Boomer entrepreneurs creating products and services for Boomers.

Now factor in the universities with marketing and entrepreneurship programs using Baby Boomers as a target market exercise. I receive dozens of e-mails a year from students who are taking classes in marketing, advertising, entrepreneurship, and product development:

> I am a senior business student at Arizona State University, and involved in a project called Innovation Space at the university. Our goal is to design a product, or modify an existing one, that improves the daily lives of the people in the baby boom generation . . .

> I am an MBA student at the Richard Ivey School of Business in London, Ontario, Canada. I am currently doing a project on a new business idea. Specifically, a travel product aimed at Baby Boomers . . .

The reason for all this activity is because there's big money to be made with products aimed at the 50-plus market. Contrary to popular belief, colleges and universities often take pragmatic approaches when creating curriculum.

A little help for entrepreneurs . . .

Mary Furlong & Associates, along with the American Society on Aging and the National Council on the Aging, sponsors a Boomer Business Summit every year. This event brings together entrepreneurs, marketers, and venture capitalists. The centerpiece of the summit is a Baby Boomer business challenge, with the winner receiving a monetary prize.

Keep abreast of this. You'll be thoroughly educated about marketing, entrepreneurship, and what venture capitalists are looking for, especially when it comes to business-plan proposals focusing on the 50-plus market. If you have a product or service that meets the criteria, enter the competition.

Visit *www.maryfurlong.com* and follow the links.

Where to Spend the Money

First, you'll have to do a bit of *media planning* on your own. Is your product a good fit for a website or targeted banner ads? Does it need a brochure or a print ad in a magazine or newspaper? Are you going to tack up a flyer on the supermarket bulletin board?* All, or some, of the above?

* I'll skip TV advertising in this chapter. See chapter six where infomercials are discussed.

Then you have to think about which creatives you should use.

As a copywriter, I would love to tell you to give all your money to me. However, as a creative director and advertising strategist, and assuming that you are working with a limited budget, let me advise you to spend your money where it will count most: an advertising-trained Baby Boomer graphic artist or web designer.

I have heretical reasons for this:

- If a website, brochure or print ad isn't visually potent, then it will simply be clutter, and whatever copy there is on the page will not be read. The print ad will be skipped, the brochure not thumbed through, the website will be ignored.

- When copy is important (as it usually is), professional advertising graphic designers are trained to arrange the page so your eyes slide to the text, and you read beyond the headline. Keeping you reading is not solely the job of the copywriter, but also of the graphic designer.

- Baby Boomer graphic designers know what is visually pleasing, exciting, and meaningful to people their own ages. "Retro" might not be retro to them. "Cutting-edge" may be only noise. Certain colors and contrasts may be too jarring to older eyes, or a layout may require more contrast and definition for older eyes.

- Regardless of age and target market, a superb advertising graphic designer is just that. Consumers will remember and revisit a print ad, pick up that brochure two or three times, bookmark a website just because they like the way it makes them feel.

It will always be easier and less expensive to pull or drop in text than it will be to redesign the advertisement or web page.

I can talk about the relationship between copy and design, of the importance of creative direction, of all the inspired elements feeding off each other, but forget all that for now. If you are on a limited advertising budget, the design is the most important element. First impressions count.

Copywriting & Campaigns & Creative Direction

A good copywriter will sit you down and listen to you talk about your product or service. He or she will make you feel comfortable, ask you lots of questions, and in many cases will translate your knowledge and excitement about the product into persuasive copy. A copywriter and designer should work together to help you develop a message. Even if one or both have not had advertising experience, *listen to them.* They know their crafts. Of course, I will get advertising professionals all in a tizzy by saying this, but advertising isn't that mysterious. You may not produce a thoroughly professional campaign, but if the copywriter is a good writer and the designer is gifted, you'll be fine.

If you're comfortable with the idea, shine the light on you and the company for a few moments. Baby Boomers love to hear the *whole* story.

I Scream, You Scream, etc.

Here are two simple campaign techniques (some call it branding) that have worked with Baby Boomers. These are not the only "schools" of advertising nor the only approaches you can take with Baby Boomers. Others are discussed in later chapters. I chose these as examples because you're probably aware of the products and their advertising.

It's also a lesson in being aware of the history of your product group—and using this knowledge to your advantage. Notice how the two techniques, although vastly different, are from a common antecedent.

The Emotional Technique

Häagen-Dazs is a good example of a product marketed to Baby Boomers in the 1970s and beyond. Wonderful product, elegant packaging. The ultimate indulgence. Grown-up ice cream. Luxury ice cream. When we were kids, Good Humor ice cream was luxury ice cream. Even if the trucks didn't make it to your neighborhood, you knew all about them. The best ice cream when we were kids: Good Humor. The best now that we are adults: Häagen-Dazs.

The Just-like-us-a-bit-off-kilter Technique

Ben & Jerry's Ice Cream went in another direction. Created by a couple of slightly wacky but average guys, Ben & Jerry's is goofy-flavored ice cream. Fun ice cream. We're-still-kids ice cream for adults. They were never shy about telling their story: a couple of knockabouts open up an ice cream shop in Vermont and have a blast experimenting with odd flavors and tossing weird candy into their concoctions.

These are two different approaches, but you can trace both back to Baby Boomers' affection for Good Humor ice cream. Good Humor was special, "the best ice cream," *and* it was "fun" ice cream with unusual flavors and playful ingredients.

Do a bit of research. Unless your product or service is something new under the sun, it has an antecedent. Consciously or not, Häagen-Dazs and Ben & Jerry's each tapped into the dual ethos of a product we cherished as kids.

The Wrong Lesson, The Right Lesson

The points I've made with the examples above have little to do with content and more to do with technique and imaging. Your product may not be snooty like Häagen-Dazs. Perhaps it's earthy and sensible. Instead of being luxurious, it could be the ultimate in practicality.

Ben Cohen and Jerry Greenfield present themselves as fun, screw-ball characters—and tell their stories. Your story and product may not be fun and wacky. But chances are it's a good story. It may be a slightly serious story, a story of hard work and perseverance, an environmentally friendly story, a story about filling a need, or one of quaint serendipity. *Just so it's a story.*

A good writer and graphic designer will make your story more interesting and accessible to a consumer.

After you are relatively happy with your copywriter and graphic designer, the next step is as important as all the thinking, research, interviewing, and hiring you've done to advertise your product: *Now leave them alone.*

CHAPTER EIGHTEEN

Now Leave Them Alone

> We think we will never know as much about a product as a client. After all, he sleeps and breathes his product . . . We couldn't possibly know as much about it as he does. By the same token, we firmly believe that he can't know as much about advertising. Because we live and breathe that all day long.
>
> —Bill Bernbach[1]

Throughout this book I have been advising advertisers and marketers to use proactive measures when dealing with ad agencies: make sure they target Baby Boomers, and when they do insist that they hire Baby Boomer creatives. I've received plenty of flack for merely hinting at these heresies in a handful of articles over the last few years. However, client interference should stop once the creative process begins.

Step Aside

At a certain point you should let your agency or freelancers take over. Of course you should always be available to them. They will need to ask questions and gather facts.

But give them plenty of breathing room. Here's why:

Whether you or they are aware of it, the target market for an advertising agency in the beginning stages of a business relationship is the client. *Agencies are selling themselves to you; they are not selling the product.* Mock campaigns have targeted *you*. (And if the initial

---

1 Denis Higgins, *The Art of Writing Advertising* (New York: McGraw-Hill, 2003).

samples have been convincing, they must be pretty good at their jobs.)*

I have learned that trying to guess what the boss or the client wants is the most debilitating of all influences in the creation of good advertising.

—Leo Burnett[2]

* Personally, I'm a bit wary about developing mock campaigns for potential clients. I don't like doing it—I've been around long enough to know that's what I'm doing, targeting the client, not the customer. For ad agencies it's *de rigueur*, but I would pay more attention to an agency's past work.

For the actual campaign, you must step aside. Account execs and creatives have to refocus. While they have plenty of experience doing this, it doesn't make their jobs easier to have the client on their minds or in their faces. Let them concentrate on the product and the consumer.

One of two things will happen if you don't. And both will have the same disastrous outcome:

1. Before long, the creatives will subconsciously ease back into a more comfortable frame of mind, targeting the client instead of the consumer. The aim of the campaign will be to glorify the product. *They'll continue to sell the product to you, not the consumer.* Often, account execs, creative directors, and creatives don't even know they're doing it. You'll end up with a print ad, a TV spot, a website that makes you feel all warm and fuzzy and proud of yourself—a real vanity piece. But it says nothing to consumers. It may even turn them off.

2. More seasoned creatives will just get fed up. They're being paid by you, so they'll give you what you want. They'll be happy to convince you that you have a great product, and that you should buy it.

I used to fall into the first category, until I realized what I was doing. Now I'm well entrenched in the second category. I *know* what I'm doing when I give up and simply make the client happy. I've made a lot of them ecstatic over the years.

---

2 Leo Burnett, 100 LEO's, (Chicago, IL: Leo Burnett Company, 1995).

At least until their products don't sell or their companies tank. But what do I care? I've been paid. Of course, these vanity campaigns won't make it to my resume or portfolio.

Okay. The truth is this: I *do* care. But after awhile you learn to simply move on to the next account.

Better advertising people than Yours Truly will find the above statement cynical. I describe these colleagues as "better" because they believe that their jobs include assuaging situations where the client is mucking up the development of campaigns.

An account executive or a creative director has convinced you to let his or her agency handle the advertising of your product. *Don't make them have to convince you again.* Stay out of the ad agency's way until they're ready to present a well-mounted campaign to you.

And If You're Not a Baby Boomer, But Your Product Is for Baby Boomers . . .

Stay very far away. If I had a product or service for young adults, I would want twenty-year-olds working on my account. If I were the creative director for a product or service targeting twenty-year-olds, I would make sure most or all of my creatives were in their twenties, and I would defer to them on almost every creative decision.

I'd be stupid not to.

CHAPTER NINETEEN

How to Critique Advertising Campaigns
for Baby Boomers

The more informative your advertising, the more persuasive
it will be.

—David Ogilvy[1]

IF YOU ARE a new entrepreneur or business owner and have yet to
see an advertising campaign or website for a product of yours, be prepared for a shock. It may be a good shock or a bad shock, but a shock
it will be.

Advertising campaigns should not be evaluated while still spinning
and crackling from the initial physiological jolt. Let it wear off.

A Negative Reaction

Culled from the quote by William Bernbach in the previous chapter:
"[The client] *sleeps and breathes his product.*" It's only natural that an
outsider's take on your product might seem off kilter. It's not how *you*
envisioned it being presented in the marketplace. Interlopers have
usurped it and are having their way with it. Give yourself and the
agency or freelancers a few days' peace. Pick up the proposed ad every
so often. Click on the website when you're not busy, but don't spend
too much time studying it.

Eventually, you'll probably discover some wonderful nuggets in the
campaign. You'll remember things you liked: pieces of copy, certain
colors, designs. If a few elements still annoy you, they can be modi-

---

1 David Ogilvy, *Confessions of an Advertising Man* (New York: Ballantine Books, 1971).

fied. In three or four days you'll probably know if it's right or if it's wrong.

Leaning towards "right?" Give the benefit of the doubt to the agency or creatives you've hired.

A Positive Reaction

It's the first time you've seen your product heralded in an ad. You eagerly zip though the copy, ogle the wondrous pictures, breathlessly romp around the website. It's better than you had ever imagined. Your product is finally coming to life. Others (the creatives) are as excited as you are about it.

This headiness will subside. A slight depression may set in. Is your product really that wonderful? Is it being oversold? Is the advertising campaign simply fluff? A collection of vanity pieces? Merely a flattering business and product profile? After a few days, you might unearth some half-truths. They could have been from misunderstandings.* Make sure these are corrected.

> * Or, as hard as it may be to believe, copywriters have been known to fiddle with the truth now and then.

Chances are that your first, second, third, and forth reactions to an initial campaign proposal will be a combination of positive and negative. You may find that some of the negatives may not be so negative, or can, with a few tweaks, become positives, while some of the positives may require rigorous reality checks.

Not all these problems are necessarily the agency's fault. Perhaps you've oversold your product to the agency or freelancer. It's healthy to be excited about a project you have dedicated your life to for a period of time. Personally, I'd rather work with people who are pumped up about their products or services than clients who nonchalantly toss something on my desk and say, "So how can we sell this?"

Give me a pumped up client. His or her enthusiasm will rub off on me. We just have to make sure that we don't go floating off into the clouds. After all, it's a product that needs to be successfully presented to thousands (or millions) of other people. The greatest campaign ever created will never make them as thrilled about the product as we are. We will be selling it. They have to be convinced to buy it. There's a big difference.

However, advertising and marketing people may be the first group of outsiders to be exposed to your product or service. On one level, we are analyzing it professionally, but on another level we're simply being human, and looking over your product as a potential customer would. *If we have questions and maybe some suggestions, listen.*

Specifically Targeting Baby Boomers

I haven't done too much self-censorship with this book (although I have no idea what my publishers will yank out!). The only thing I'm trying *not* to do is be the invasive, albeit absent creative director. Every so often I've slipped up (and probably will continue to do so in succeeding chapters). I simply want to suggest some guidelines, offer some insights. If you follow my advice and hire Baby Boomer creatives, you'll be playing the odds, and more than likely end up with an effective campaign.

Below are a few things to keep in mind when evaluating advertising and marketing collateral targeting Baby Boomers. If any of these pop out at you, bring them up. However, it could be that your creative director, copywriter, or graphic designer will have good reasons why they did what they did.

I trust them. So should you.

Design

- If your print ad or web page looks too glossy, Baby Boomers might be turned off. Our eyes are more sensitive to bright light. We've lost a bit of color perception abilities. So make sure the basic design isn't full of glaring whites and limp pastels. (Unless, of course, your product or service has something to do with the decades of the Fifties or Seventies.)

- More often than not, the feel should be rich and deep. but with elements well delineated.

- Fonts should be larger than normal, but not insultingly so. I've often seen ads targeting 50-plus consumers with print Mr. Magoo could speed-read.

- If it's a website, make sure it isn't too busy. We're not looking to be overwhelmed, just whelmed. If you want to include a flash presentation, make it simple and quick.

- Baby Boomers are web savvy. Don't dumb down the navigation and design, but also don't turn it into a virtual funhouse or amusement park ride.

Copy

- Headlines and copy should not be full of hype, but simple and declarative. No exclamation marks. It's partly our ages; Baby Boomers have seen it all. We don't appreciate carnival barkers. Just tell us what's in the tent.

- Contrary to what you are told by a few so-called generational marketing experts, Baby Boomers do not think that they are still in their teens and twenties. We do not need to be grabbed immediately by an advertisement. We're not fidgety toddlers with limited attention spans, or frazzled white rabbits running around aimlessly.

- Don't be afraid to ease Baby Boomers into your advertisement or website. We have the time, and if you can supply the interest, we'll be interested. Baby Boomers want to know as much as possible about the product or service.

- Whether print or electronic media, tell a story. Make it a seamless narrative involving the product, the company, and the benefits to the consumer. The person who invented it and the company that manufactures it are just as important as the shiny new product you are selling.

Baby Boomers are old enough to look back on our lives, but young enough to have plenty of time to plan, look forward to, or fantasize a productive, meaningful future. We relate to products that have stories because *we* have stories, and our stories are far from over. If we come across a product that has a history, we will identify with it, and presume it has a future. A product that appears out of nowhere, that seems to have been spontaneously hatched from the ether, is not as enticing. It may have been enticing to us twenty-five or more years ago, and it may still be enticing to teens and twenty-somethings, but not to us. *Give us a story where the protagonist (your product) is approaching the prime of its life.*

What will drive Baby Boomers *away* is blatant hucksterism and ballyhoo. Don't introduce an innovative safety pin as if it were a cure for cancer.

Personally, I'd be interested in a safer safety pin. I've been pricked too many times by nametags given to me at conventions, symposiums and trade shows. If there's a better safety pin out there, I want to know about it. But if the material this pin is made out of is presented to me as the most important metallurgical advance since smelting, and if you tell me that the fastening features exceed the safety requirements for all NASA moon-walking spacesuits, my eyes will glaze over and I'll turn the page. I'll probably never know it's a pretty good safety pin.

Don't Micromanage the Campaign

There will always be changes you will want to make, and some you will have to make. But keep those changes to only information that is incorrect about your product or service. Don't start rewriting and redesigning.

If good writers have never written any advertising copy in their lives, they are still good writers. Writers know how to structure sentences for readability, how to create rhythms within phrases, sentences, and paragraphs. They can tell stories and create word pictures.

Designers know how to keep your focus where it should be, and what colors and layouts evoke the best ambiance for your campaign. If you do not like the color scheme, have them change the color scheme. Don't tell them which hues, tints, and shadings to use with the agreed color scheme.

Fiddling with the good is as bad as leaving in the not so good. While the following quote refers to advertising creatives—specifically copywriters—I would also apply it to advertisers critiquing campaigns. Inspired first-drafts are often diluted in revisions by well-meaning clients or marketing executives trying to "improve" or "add something" to campaigns:

> I have learned that any fool can write a bad ad, but it takes a real genius to keep his hands off a good one.
>
> —Leo Burnett[2]

If creatives can muck up their own work, think what damage *you* can do to it. By the same token, if a creative has changed an ad on his or her own, and you liked the original draft, don't be afraid to mention it.

---

2 Leo Burnett, *100 LEO's*, (Chicago, IL: Leo Burnett Company, 1995).

PART III

Some Resources, A Case Study,
and Final Thoughts

CHAPTER TWENTY

The Branding Circus

The truth is, we've always overestimated the power of branding while underestimating consumers' ability to recognize quality.

—James Surowiecki[1]

A Tongue-in-Cheek History of Advertising and the Cyclical Apocalypse

BEGINNING in the early twentieth century, it was all sales and advertising. With the introduction of branding, advertising gained enough influence and power to become a major player, breaking away from sales and creating its own industry. Marketing was in its infancy, a middleman between advertising and sales.

When mass media came along (radio mostly), buckets of marketing were tossed into the brew. In the late 1950s and certainly by the end of the 1960s, demographics became a major star. It bolstered marketing's assets. However, no one was sure whether marketing should be a subset of sales or a subset of advertising.

Marketing fooled them both. Advertising and sales became subsets of *marketing*.

Always around but keeping a low profile was Public Relations.

Over the last ten or fifteen years, three concurrent forces have changed everything. I'm not sure if they meant to work together, or knew they were working together, but they *did* work together:

1. Multinational marketing and advertising conglomerates came

1 "The Decline of Brands," *Wired* Magazine, November 2004

into being by merging or buying other marketing, advertising, and public relations firms.

2. Cable and satellite TV, the internet, the growth of specialty magazines, and a few other technologically advanced funnels recharged marketing, creating a new star: *Media Planning*.

3. As these two revolutions roiled, a sturdy, reliable advertising workhorse became a bit bloated and bossy: *Branding*.

Not sure if it wanted it, and not even sure what it would do with it if it got it, marketing tried to steal branding away from advertising. Advertising fought back. But branding fooled them both. Advertising and marketing became subsets of *branding*.

Don't read on if you have a weak stomach.

Branding ate its young, *and* its old, eventually mutating into an insatiable hydra-headed monster. Today, marketing is around merely to create Brands. Advertising to nurture Brands. Media Planning to disperse Brands. Public Relations to protect and defend Brands. And the oddest of all: Products are around simply to feed Brands.

There are no products anymore, just strange images (perhaps just *feelings*) that you go to the store and buy. Inside the packages are usually some sort of products. But that's not really what's important. The only thing that matters is this: You've bought *The Brands*.

Yes, I'm having fun, being flippant—but how wrong am I?

And if I'm not wrong, how long will this Orwellian branding spectacle last? Is today's branding economically advantageous for the advertiser? Especially advertisers who want to target Baby Boomers?

I work with, and talk to, all sorts of people in advertising, marketing, public relations, media planning, and so on. It used to be that all these people were specialists in their fields. Copywriters wrote copy, designers designed, print media marketers were print media marketers, television marketers were television marketers. When working together, we had our own *métiers*. We complemented each other.

Of course, we each knew a fair-to-significant amount about the other fields. Often we would become proficient in these disciplines. Some of us changed disciplines, often becoming two-gun gunslingers.

Not any more. Now we are (or had better be) all experts on *brand-ing*—and branding *only*. To be understood (and to be taken seriously) we must all speak branding *language*. We'd better all be sorcerers conjuring up mystical, subliminal, atavistic, symbolic something-or-others.

The One-Ring Circus

I've been hearing a lot of talk lately about how to "break through the clutter" so your brand stands out. This is double-talk. Substitute the word "branding" for "clutter." These people want to convince you that the way to break through the branding is to create more branding. Make any sense to you?

But you *should* listen to me. I can break through the clutter for you. It's easy.

Going back to my dental aisle example in a previous chapter, I would advise a toothpaste client to create packaging that is plain white, with merely the word TOOTHPASTE emboldened on the package. (A big secret everybody knows: All the so-called generic brands aren't generic anymore. They've hopped on the "branding bandwagon.")*

> * There are *brands* of generics now, and even coordinated campaigns for generic products and companies offering generic products. Sort of defeats the purpose, don't you think?

I guarantee that this plain white packaging will break though the clutter. I can also pretty much guarantee that not too many people will buy your product. But they'll see it. However, be forewarned: If I'm wrong, and by some miracle this toothpaste *does* fly off the shelves, then everybody will begin packaging their toothpastes in plain wrapping, and yours won't be breaking through the clutter anymore.

Some other branding expert will have a *new* solution for you, though.

What is Branding?

One of the reasons it's so difficult to define branding is because in the advertising and marketing world the term is so invasive, so ubiquitous, that it has lost all of its original meaning.

Ask six people to define what "Branding" is and you will get seven different answers. The longer I've been in the business, the truer this has become. Perhaps it's time to pull the plug.

—Hugh Macleod[2]

Branding is only one of many elements in the advertising and marketing arsenal—and perhaps the least important when you are initially fashioning a campaign. When you release a new product, advertising sets the stage for brand recognition to sink in: a good logo, copy with short, memorable phrases, and so forth. These branding techniques are used along with all other advertising elements.

Test marketing isn't going to tell you if your initial branding techniques will be successful. If there is some sort of mystical, subliminal value in branding, you won't find it out during controlled studies. Branding takes time. You won't know what you have or what you'll need until it's out and about for a while. That's because the soul of branding is the relationship that develops between the customer and the product. It's not something that can be whipped up out of thin air. There is no magic "branding wand" that you wave over a new advertising campaign before it's picked up by messenger for a sprint to the printer, digitally dashes through the ether to newspapers and magazines, or is whisked away by FedEx to local television stations.

Attempting to brand your product before it's been in the marketplace for a period of time is a waste of time. So if someone tells you that you have to brand your product immediately, ignore him.

A Bit of Research and Some Lifts and Tucks

Once your product has been sloshing around for a while in the marketplace, user focus groups can come in handy. You can refashion your branding.

The simplest of simple examples: If your logo is full of angles and bright colors, but your product is being perceived as warm and cuddly, maybe those angles should be softened, those colors muted. If your product is causing excitement and is on everybody's lips, but your

2 *Gapingvoid.com*, Hugh Macleod's creative advertising blog, September, 2004

logo is soft and curvy, think about using more vibrant colors and turn those curves into sharp angles. Make it crackle.

Personally (and if it's possible) I prefer to talk to people about products. If I know someone uses a product, I ask him why he bought it, ask why he likes it, and so on. The more casual the setting, the better the responses are likely to be. But if you have to get by with focus groups, fine.

David Wolfe has written an excellent book: *Ageless Marketing*. (In the next chapter, I talk more about it.) I might argue with some of his fine points, even some of his commanding ones, but his general concepts about marketing are learned, fascinating, and touch on the profound.

In one section of *Ageless Marketing*, Mr. Wolfe analyzes the success of New Balance® as a brand and product in the 45-plus market. After reading his book (and his blog) I started asking Baby Boomers wearing New Balance shoes why they liked them.

It takes a bit of cajoling to get people to talk because they think I'm nuts for asking. They become even more convinced of my precarious mental state as I continually bombard them with questions about why they purchase certain products over others. After awhile they just assume I'm a harmless fruitcake, and yack away.

The New Balance answers:

> They're the most comfortable.

> I can always find my size.

> When I go into a shoe store I usually say to myself, "OK, I'm going to try on a bunch of shoes. If I can't find anything I like, or anything that fits perfectly, I can always get a pair of New Balance." I know they'll fit and be comfortable.

Of course, new shoes are rarely comfortable. They may *become* comfortable after you wear them for a few days, but that's not the point. After trying on so many pairs of shoes (it's not the "event" it once was when you were younger), you're ready to get out of there, and *anything* seems comfortable. Plus, they've already convinced themselves that New Balance will be the last shoes they will tuck their feet into. It's almost a relief to do so.

But my favorite response was this:

"I buy them because they're not too ugly."

For me, the quote above is the story in a nutshell. I'm not suggesting that New Balance should use this as a campaign cornerstone:

Buy New Balance. Because They're Not Too Ugly.

However, if they do use it I can sue them and be able to retire, or at least buy a second car, or a couple of pairs of Keds or PF Flyers, since Baby Boomers don't change brands. My point is that this is precious advertising fodder, and while coming from a different perspective than David Wolfe's trenchant treatise on New Balance's branding, it does not contradict what he has to say.

Whatever marketing techniques you use to gather information, that information will help you *brand* your product. That's what branding is. It's a laborious process. After a product is tossed into the marketplace, you analyze the positive and negative reactions of consumers. Branding is an effort to reflect that positive relationship the consumer *now* has with the product by refashioning the product's logo, copy, design, and message, along with adjusting any target marketing. At some point the logo will sink in and will then have some meaning to consumers. In the beginning, it means nothing.

Branding experts pass themselves off as magicians. The problem is that the tricks may impress you when you first see them, but once you're out of the theatre you can't even remember what the tricks were, or, in most cases, what the products were.

What Branding is Today

Branding now isn't branding at all. It's merely hoopla, a big show, a big logo in the sky. Branding's most important element, the continuing relationship between the consumer and the product, is lost amidst the promotional clutter. Breaking through the clutter won't do much of anything.

Baby Boomers are especially immune to such shenanigans, and have been for some time. If we like a product, we'll buy it, and a relationship may or may not develop. If it does, we will personally endorse it when talking to friends. If it becomes a part of our lives, we'll probably dig deeper into the values of the product and we may become a bit cultish about it.* But all this isn't going to happen because of a branding campaign for a product we know nothing about and have never used.

> * There are even some branding experts who study cults—trying to figure out why people join cults so they can create "instant cults" with their initial branding campaigns. This is how desperate they've become.

I'll be branded as a whistle-blower, a troublemaker, but all branding is today is advertising. It's the new word for advertising, and not a very good one. Due to fractured, varied target markets, and the scores of new ways to reach consumers, branding has become the easiest way of dealing with all the variables. It's a dumbed-down version of advertising. You could call it *instant* advertising—something that has no lasting value to the consumer, or to the advertiser. It's a quick fix.

In show biz parlance, the hydra-headed branding monster has no legs.

> Fundamentally, people armed with information make decisions of self-interest. This is not *The Manchurian Candidate*, where they're responding to messages buried deep within their psyche that they don't even know are there. There's a lot of people in the advertising industry who would like it to be that way, and there's a lot of people outside of the advertising industry who imagine it to be that way, but it ain't that way.
>
> —Bob Garfield, "The Persuaders," PBS *Frontline*[3]

> Like many things, being successful in advertising to Boomers will only come to those who get the details right. . . . Ads with more product information will work better than ads that skimp on the specifics.
>
> —Matt Thornhill, The Boomer Project[4]

---

3 Bob Garfield, *Ad Age* magazine columnist, interviewed on PBS *Frontline's* "The Persuaders"

4 *www.boomerproject.com*

I'm guessing that the branding circus is about over. It will return, for advertising techniques are as cyclical as most everything in life seems to be. Print copywriting was once King, the radio commercial was once King, the television commercial was once King. Now, the brightly colored, crackles-and-explodes-in-your-mouth, rather tasteless and nutritiously deficient branding message is King.

But not for much longer.

My Tongue-Somewhat-in-Cheek Dire Prediction

The next hydra-headed monster? With apologies to my good friends and associates in this field, it could be *Public Relations*. PR used to be smiley faces. Today it's become a lifeline for many products that have gotten themselves into trouble. Like branding, PR is now considered something you do with your product *before* it's tossed into the marketplace. PR has grown, evolved, and some of the smartest people I know are in public relations, but . . . advertising, marketing, and sales could all end up as subsets of public relations.

My fear is that all the various marketing and advertising disciplines lose their power, focus, and identities when one becomes too powerful.

I love New Balance shoes. But in the advertising industry, it's time for some *old* balance.

CHAPTER TWENTY-ONE

Some Useful Resources in Books

TODAY'S BABY BOOMERS marketing boom was preceded (and predicted) by scores of business professionals and sociologists. More books will be released and articles written as the movement continues for the next twenty-five or more years.

I haven't (and probably won't) read them all. Truth is, I go out of my way *not* to read every book about marketing and advertising. As David Wolfe stresses in *Ageless Marketing*, our values and priorities change as we age, and I read enough advertising and marketing tomes in my teens, twenties, and thirties to fill a Pepsi Challenge tour bus.

Some of the good ones I've read recently:

Marketing to Leading-Edge Baby Boomers
by Brent Green

Brent grasps the dichotomy between young and old Boomers. If you market to boomers and just play the "forever young" card, you're in big trouble. Likewise, if you treat us only as people getting old, you've lost us again.

Brent's practical approach, by using examples of actual marketing and advertising campaigns, explains to marketers and advertisers what works and what doesn't. He coaches advertising creatives how to fuse concepts that on the surface appear to be mutually exclusive. Boomers want to hear something most of us already know: What makes us fun, meaningful, and productive is accepting and relishing the variety in our lives.

Many standard Baby Boomer advertising concepts are turned upside down in the book. One of my favorites is a warning about using some of the great recordings from the Sixties and early Seventies for commercial campaigns. It's only a warning, and in certain instances this technique works just fine.

But be cautious. My take on it is that this is not always a good idea. Those classic recordings already have a visceral stamp. To merge them with new images can create cognitive dissonance. Sure, they grab your attention at first, but then you're off in some warped, cozy daydream, and the last thing on your mind is what you're watching. (However, I do like thinking that Richie Havens, Etta James, or whoever the members of the Strawberry Alarm Clock were are probably getting chunky checks in the mail.)

Brent talks wisely about using earlier pop music from the late Fifties and early Sixties. Why? Read his book.

*56 percent of Boomers feel the country needs a strong third political party.[1]

Brent also considers what we might be like when we really *do* get old. He and Yours Truly share the same prediction: with time on our hands, we may very well become ornery activists, or at the very least a vibrant bunch of crotchety troublemakers.*

In the new paperback second edition of *Marketing to Leading-Edge Baby Boomers,* (Paramount Market Publishing, 2006), Brent has added a large section about copywriting. He's one of those two-gun gunslingers I've talked about previously, someone who is equally adept at marketing and advertising.

50+ Marketing
by Jean-Paul Tréguer

It is not easy to communicate with the over 50s. They are demanding consumers, given to skepticism and not likely to be deceived by tricks.

—Jean-Paul Tréguer

That statement should strike fear in the hearts of all marketing and advertising folks. But do you want to hear something even scarier?

The future is frankly not rosy for young people in the

---

1 AARP Study, *www.seniorjournal.com*

coming years. They will become increasingly isolated in the middle of a flood of silver-haired people.

—Jean-Paul Tréguer

No, Jean-Paul is not some "doom and gloom" futurist or crackpot science fiction writer, but a seasoned advertising executive and founder of the highly successful International Senior-agency® with offices in London, Brussels, Hamburg, Oslo, Paris, Stockholm, Vienna, and Sydney. However, his impressive team of professionals does suggest a sci-fi/horror flick titled, *Invasion of the Advertising Agency Talent Snatchers.* They've been plucked from top-notch outfits Saatchi & Saatchi, BMP/DDB, Ogilvy & Mather, and others.

Jean-Paul's advertising philosophy is simple, but not always easily understood, and certainly not put to use as often as it should be. It's called Generational Marketing. GM suggests that you market to specific generations, not to demographic age brackets. The shared experiences and culture of each generation will be the defining marketing and advertising fodder as generations get older.

For example, you don't market to the WWII generation as late-sixty to early-eighty year-olds. You reach them by analyzing and emphasizing their lifelong experiences and how these experiences shaped them; what they went through during the Depression as youngsters, WWII as teens and young adults, the Fifties as parents, all the way up to today as retired grandparents. Likewise, you don't market to Baby Boomers based on the fact that they are now in their late forties and fifties. You factor in their culture and shared experiences.

The same basic marketing concepts for each generation will carry you (the advertiser or marketer or advertising creative) through all age brackets. Don't think that what holds true now for marketing to Baby Boomers will hold true for GenX when they reach their fifties.

Jean-Paul Tréguer's insights and practical advice cover everything from mass media to product ergonomics and packaging. He's a big believer in the infomercial, and while I've yet to see an infomercial produced in the U.S. that has convinced me to buy anything, I also know that the form isn't the problem; the content is.*

* See chapter six in this book about Infomercials.

Ageless Marketing
by David B. Wolfe

Any marketing book that opens with a healthy amount of disdain for bean counters will suck me in immediately. And any marketing book (any book, actually) that references Isaac Newton, William Shakespeare, Carl Jung, Konstantin Stanislavski (the Russian theatre director and acting teacher), and Stephen Jay Gould will keep my toes wiggling.

Only one aggregate of numbers means much to Mr. Wolfe:

For the first time ever, most adults are 40 or older. This New Customer Majority has radically changed the rules of marketplace engagement because its members see life through a different lens than younger consumers who once determined the rules.

In 2000, (The New Customer Majority) was 45% larger than the 18–39 age group (123 to 85 million), by 2010 it will be 61% larger: 138 to 86 million money-spending consumers.

By 2010, adults 45 and older will outspend younger adults by $1 trillion ($2.6 to $1.6 trillion).

In other words, the median age of adults will rise each over the next ten years, going from where it is today (around 45) up to the low 50s.

What about that prized, succulent 18–39 demographic advertisers salivate over? Today it's a slice; tomorrow, a sliver.

While there's a huge amount of work to be done convincing ad agencies to target David's *New Customer Majority*, once it happens, then what? How do you capture the hearts and minds of the 40-plus market?

This is where the author of *Ageless Marketing* shines. David is a true thinker. He's not convinced that generational marketing holds *all* the answers. His ageless-marketing theory incorporates profound insights and startling data from Shakespeare to cutting-edge medical techniques (MRIs). There *are* ages of man. We change. We evolve. In our middle-to-later years, we're less self-centered, more self-actualized, and have developed wider-ranging interests and priorities. If you are to reach the *New Customer Majority*, you must appeal to these values:

> While the way in which they (Baby Boomers) pursue satisfaction of their needs may differ from previous generations because of more options available, their basic needs are the same at comparable ages as their parents and grandparents.

David also talks about how these values have been incubating during our younger years, and that this is true of all generations.

I don't think David would disagree with me if I were similarly inclusive in my thinking, and tossed hefty chunks of generational marketing into the mix. I find that if someone has something intelligent and insightful to say, it never smacks of dogma, and is rarely mutually exclusive.

For me, David Wolfe's *ageless marketing* concepts keep me grounded—so I won't become too deeply immersed in generational advertising—and lose perspective.

A Whole New Mind (see below) is a good companion read with David Wolfe's *Ageless Marketing.*

77 Truths About Marketing to the 50+ Consumer
by Kurt Medina and John Migliaccio

Sure, I have a problem with anything that claims to be the "truth" about anything. A better title for this mini-tome might be: "77 Very, Very Valuable Insights That You Should Keep Close and Reference Regularly Whenever Formulating a Marketing or Advertising Campaign Where the Target Market Is Over 50 Years

Old and You Want to Reach Baby Boomers, Pre-Retirees, the Post-WWII and WWII Generations, or Any of These Demographics Individually, Collectively, or Grouped in Twos or Threes." So, *77 Truths About Marketing To The 50+ Consumer* will have to do, or there wouldn't be room on the cover for the authors' names.

Marketing Vision: What *77 Truths* isn't, is a bulky, unwieldy hardcover, read once, admired, and carefully placed on a bookshelf, never to be opened again tome. Kurt and John traded their 15 minutes of instant celebrity for something much more valuable: practical business expertise that's always available for consultation.

It's on my desk, within arm's reach at all times. Many people carry it around with them. Fame vs. Function. Do you think they've won in the long run?

PrimeTime Women: How to Win the Hearts, Minds, and Business of Boomer Big Spenders
by Marti Barletta

PrimeTime Women is a breeze to read—like sitting around with Ms. Barletta, chatting. And in the room are dozens of fascinating, ready-to-rumble women, chiming in every so often. The overarching theme of *PrimeTime Women* really isn't the money they control; it's the fact that they are taking control of their lives. This is a phenomenon unique to Baby Boomers (and a bit older). After fifty is better than before fifty. There have always been a few women who bloomed in their later years. For Boomers it's become a generational ethos. The second part of the book is nuts and bolts. I was swept away by many of her "word-of-mouth" marketing paradigms. She eschews the cheesy WOM tactics so often used today in favor of real, truly inspired marketing/PR/promotional techniques.

There are hundreds of great quotes in *PrimeTime Women* (read it with your yellow highlighter handy), but if I had to pick my favorite:

PrimeTimers are not compelled to make social statements by their brand choices, and PrimeTime Women are no longer controlled by the need to have perfect looks and perfect behavior. . . . Looking for the long-submerged "secret self" is also about listening to one's own counsel rather than listening to others. PrimeTimers are more individuated, more autonomous, and less influenced by peers and celebrity endorsements.

The takeaway for me: I learned a ton and enjoyed the experience of hanging around a bunch of intelligent, creative, energetic, forward-thinking women. Even a few creative sparks went off as I read, helping me with ad concepts for my clients.

Not specifically about the 50+ Market
(but you might want to check them out anyway):

A Whole New Mind: Moving from the Information Age to the Conceptual Age
by Daniel H. Pink

A flowing, fun read about right/left brain functions. Mr. Pink suggests that a revolution will happen this century as we begin to favor right-brain modes of creativity and empathy.

Also worth reading: Dan Pink's article in *Wired*, "What Kind of Genius Are You?" is about genius—dispelling more than a few myths about creativity primarily being the property of the young:

> A new theory suggests that creativity comes in two distinct types—quick and dramatic, or careful and quiet. . . . What he (David Galenson, University of Chicago) has found is that genius—whether in art or architecture or even business—is not the sole province of 17-year-old Picassos and 22-year-old Andreessens. Instead, it comes in two very different forms, embodied by two very different types of people. "Conceptual innovators," as Galenson calls them, make bold, dramatic leaps in their disciplines. They do their breakthrough work when they are young. Think Edvard Munch, Herman Melville, and Orson Welles. They make the rest of us feel like

also-rans. Then there's a second character type, someone who's just as significant but trudging by comparison. Galenson calls this group "experimental innovators." Geniuses like Auguste Rodin, Mark Twain, and Alfred Hitchcock proceed by a lifetime of trial and error and thus do their important work much later in their careers. Galenson maintains that this duality—conceptualists are from Mars, experimentalists are from Venus—is the core of the creative process. And it applies to virtually every field of intellectual endeavor, from painters and poets to economists.[1]

And while sniffing around Dan's website (*www.danpink.com*) I found this:

> *Science News* reports on a study that says an aging brain may be a more emotionally astute brain. "Advancing age heralds a growth in emotional stability accompanied by a neural transition to increased control over negative emotions and greater accessibility of positive emotions," the story says. By contrast, people under 50 can access negative emotions more quickly and easily than positive ones. "This gradual reorganization of the brain's emotion system may result from older folk responding to accumulating personal experiences by increasingly looking for meaning in life."

Get Back in the Box
by Douglas Rushkoff

It's tough to corral this one is a tight paragraph. Rushkoff bolts off in dozens of directions, taking us on explosive, cerebral fun rides. But his overarching message is a conservative one: getting back to core values with products/services and eschewing wacky, empty branding techniques.

---

1 Dan Pink, "What Kind of Genius Are You?" *Wired* Magazine, Issue 14.07, July 2006

Tribal Knowledge
by John Moore

If you're in business merely to sell any product or service, and you need to be kicked in the ass by all sorts of empty motivational fodder and marketing department rave-ups, *Tribal Knowledge* probably won't make much sense to you. You'd be better off reading books with titles like "HOW TO SELL ANYTHING TO ANYBODY" or "GET ON OPRAH and MAKE A $MILLION$ DOLLARS IN ONE (Yes, I said one!) MONTH."

However, if you're genuinely passionate about your offering, whether you're an entrepreneur tinkering in a garage or the CMO of a multinational, this book is for you.

I have a number of clients with passion for their products/services. Actually, most have it. But they don't know what to do with it. Some are embarrassed by their passion, and opt for a straight-laced, too-tight-tie approach. They don't want anybody to think that they're out of control. It wouldn't be very business-like. Then there are the unbridled enthusiasts who overwhelm you with their bubbly chatter. Often their excitement just gets in the way of getting down to business. Uptight or gushy, these are the people who are often business visionaries.

But being a business visionary and getting your vision off the ground, and keeping it hovering—first over three or four places, then over thousands—are two (or three, or four) very different things.

John Moore tells the story of Howard Shultz and Starbucks, and how the company funneled its passion (not only for a great cup of coffee but *for the experience* of a great cup of coffee) into a practical marketing plan. John says that the company kept reinvesting its profits. True. But between the lines you realize that what they really did was reinvest their passion. Over and over. Until... well, you know what happened.

Tribal Knowledge is primary source material. John worked there. He also worked for Whole Foods. These are two companies that created their own industries—not quite out of thin air, but almost. So listen to him.

What's to Glean from Reading Marketing Books, and What to be Wary About

Again, I'm guessing that many people raking through these pages will be entrepreneurs, merchants, and businesspeople with a product or service appropriate for Baby Boomers (which means just about every product for the general public). If you're already familiar with marketing and advertising books, skip the next few pages.

Marketing and advertising books aren't much different from most other kinds of business or advice books. Some are written by bright people and some by not-so-bright people, visionaries and hucksters, folks with practical advice, others with theoretical advice. However, most are written by professionals who simply want to pass on what they've learned. Sure, many are looking for a sliver of glory. Nothing wrong with that.

There are also a dozen or so Marketing Gurus. You won't have to look very hard to find them.

Being a bit jaded and skeptical by nature, I don't have a guru. You might want to latch on to one, and that's fine. Some people do better when they have a plan to stick to, when rules and procedures are plainly laid out. Many of these gurus have plenty of fascinating things to say, both practical and theoretical. I'm deeply impressed with a handful of them. A few I can do without.

I'm just not much of a follower. So when someone tells me (in so many words) that he has found a marketing or advertising guru and that this guru's way is the only way, I wince. If you read a marketing or advertising book that you think is great, and want to keep reading about these disciplines, do it. *But pick a book by another author.* Skip the handful of books by the author you've just read, and the various articles the author may have written, or you might end up a tad brainwashed.

The more books and articles you read about these subjects, the more you'll realize that many of the theories and practices put forth are by no means mutually exclusive. You can soak up valuable advice from scores of sources.

You may also want to find a history book of advertising or marketing to give you a bit of perspective. Here's a good example from the past:

The Old Days—The Old, Old Days—and Today

Back in the 50s and 60s, advertising held sway over marketing. There were many more Advertising Gurus than Marketing Gurus. Two giants at the time were David Ogilvy and Rosser Reeves. There were others, but to make my story simple, I'll just stick with these two.

Of course, these two gurus had their own (multiple) gurus:

> If you want the (Copywriters) Hall of Fame to be a true Hall of Fame, and if in the course of this ceremony you are going to pick great campaigns, then I think you're going to have to go back into history and get some of the immortal copywriters now dead, like Wilbur Ruthrauff, John Kennedy, Claude Hopkins, Sterling Getchell, O. B. Winders, Sid Schwinn—and give them gold keys for the great historic campaigns that changed the face of this business. The evidence is all in on those campaigns. They really worked. Their campaigns are monolithic monuments.
>
> —Rosser Reeves[2]

David Ogilvy and Rosser Reeves had their respective fanatical followers. For awhile, there was an internecine industry culture war. Ogilvy had a more individual, creative approach to advertising:

> I have a theory that the best ads come from personal experience. Some of the good ones I have done have really come out of the real experience of my life, and somehow this has come over as true and valid and persuasive.
>
> —David Ogilvy[3]

2, 3 Denis Higgins, *The Art of Writing Advertising* (New York: McGraw-Hill, 2003).

Reeves was more clinical. He came up with something all advertising folks know as USP (Unique Selling Proposition): Find out what is unique about your product and push that. What makes M&Ms different than all other candies? Reeves came up with, "Melts in Your Mouth, Not in Your Hand."

While these two giants were rivals (and at one time brothers-in-law), Reeves once admitted:

> David Ogilvy and I, strangely enough, see almost eye to eye. His techniques are different from mine. . . . But if you look at the advertising of the two agencies, you would discover that David and I are operating on the same principles.[4]

The debate still rages about the philosophies and techniques of Ogilvy and Reeves. I don't debate this stuff. I've learned from both. (And about fifty others.) There are at least twenty-five books about targeting the 40-plus market (and two or three gurus). You certainly don't have to read them all, but you should read a few, or a handful. Then incorporate the ideas you like and feel comfortable with when working with your advertising agency or freelancer.

However, if enough people who read *this* book start believing that all the words on these pages are *pure gold*, that *my* advertising wisdom is divinely inspired, then I may start a cult and commune. I'll have my followers hand over all their worldly goods; early each morning we'll join in an "advertising to Baby Boomers" ritual breakfast, afterward I'll send them all out into the business world to preach the *Advertising to Baby Boomers Gospel of Chuck*, and I'll play golf for the rest of the day.

Just be careful. Advertising and marketing folks know how to weave spells better than most. Find yourself *many* gurus.

And . . . if you believe that all the words in this book are merely gilt-edged, send me golf balls.

---

4 Ibid.

CHAPTER TWENTY-TWO

Interview with Kevin Lavery of Millennium

MILLENNIUM GROUP is an ad agency in the U.K. with 200 employees. That alone won't get any hearts pounding or eyes bulging. So here's the kicker: *Millennium only takes on clients that want to target the 50+ market.*

Are there any comparable agencies on this side of the pond? Yeah, mine, less 199 employees. Sure, it's only me and the dog and the cat— but I do have a dozen or so top-notch creatives and marketing folks whom I call upon when needed. We get things done. Any others? There is a handful of small (very small) agencies focusing on the mature market, and one large agency with a mature market division and a handful of employees. That's about it.

Kevin Lavery is co-founder and Executive Creative Director of Millennium. We chatted at a business conference in Chicago at the end of 2006. Of course, I grilled him. My first question was why he and his partner Martin Smith thought they could get a 50+ ad agency off the ground. Did they have clients he knew about who were looking for experts in the field, or was it just a hunch?

"Forming Millennium was Martin Smith's idea," Kevin said. "He was marketing director for an organization called Saga, which provides many services from vacations to financial services to people over fifty. Saga's magazine has a circulation of over one million, and he realized that the older demographic was going to be hugely important. Also he had always wanted to start an agency—fool!"

Kevin backtracked a bit. "In 1980, I co-founded a direct-response ad agency (Lavery Rowe Advertising). I sold my interest in the early 1990s," he said, "and was looking around for something to do. I'd been a friend and business associate with Martin. Martin felt he could make a go of establishing a 50+-focused agency but there was one problem. He hadn't formed or built an agency before, a case of optimism over experience! I, on the other hand, had. We agreed to get together and see how things would develop, with a review of the situation after three months. Well, after three months (May 1996) the signs were encouraging. As I had nothing better to do, we agreed to make our partnership permanent."

I wanted to know what "encouraging" meant. Were advertisers knocking down their doors? Kevin smiled and shook his head. He said it was simply this: the more hard research they did, the better the idea of a 50+ agency sounded to them. "We didn't really know if any specific companies were actually looking to appoint a 50+-focused agency, but we knew a lot of them would be interested in the demographics. The other slight problem was that we were only five people with no clients, so we had to sell the only thing we had—ourselves. It was a case of getting to see as many organizations as possible in the hope of picking up some projects and/or getting on pitch lists.

"Our first major breakthrough came late 1996 when we were asked to pitch for an organization called NPI (a large insurance and pension provider) who had an equity release product aimed at home-owners aged over seventy. We won the pitch hands down. One of the winning ideas became the cornerstone of its marketing and advertising for several years to come. The campaign was built around the 'ration book.' During the Second World War-years and right up until 1954, everything was rationed in the U.K. and everyone, including (allegedly) the King, had a ration book. So the premise of the campaign for NPI was: *Homeowners, retirement needn't be a return to rationing . . . you can release extra cash from your home.* The direct mail and press advertising campaign was astonishingly successful and went on to win the coveted best financial services campaign at the DMA/Royal Mail awards in 1997. In a nutshell, this was what really made Millennium take off. Soon NPI was spending nearly $2 million with us."

Kevin and Martin also relied on the raw customer data they had been collecting. "It came out of our work with NPI. When we were planning the initial direct mail campaign we asked all the major lifestyle data providers for details of all records of people over the age of seventy who owned their own homes. The response surprised us. They said no one had ever asked them for this before! Next we asked them if we could rent this data and create a data pool of names so that they could all share in the revenues. They agreed and went on to provide us with very high volumes of names for NPI and other clients. This was what prompted us to develop our own data management business which is now a very profitable part of the Millennium Group."

In 1999, Kevin Lavery wrote one of the first books about the 50+ Market, *The Definitive Guide to Grey Marketing*. "We used it as a very successful 'door opener.' Other account wins followed, notably Norwich Union, one of the U.K.'s biggest insurance and pension companies, who asked us to launch its 'retirement solutions' portfolio."

"So in the U.K., what perceptions have changed about the 50+ market since 1996? And the perception of Millennium as a valid agency?" I asked.

"What we realized in the early years was that it doesn't matter how good a story you tell to prospective clients and no matter how competent and creative your offering is, there are certain organizations who will not use you unless you reach a certain size or critical mass. In the beginning we'd spend most of the introductory (credentials) meetings explaining the demographic shift. Nowadays most people understand the importance of the 50+ market, so therefore our credentials are about how we can help clients get more out of the older consumer."

"And what about other ad agencies? Why aren't there ten 'Millenniums' in the U.K. and twenty on this side of the pond?"

"I don't think it is a deliberate ploy by marketing and advertising agencies to ignore the over 50s; rather that these agencies are made up of young people who almost subconsciously target who and what they know." ▪

Millennium online: www.millenniumdirect.co.uk *or google* "Millennium Direct + UK"

CHAPTER TWENTY-THREE

Some Useful Resources on the Web

WHEN YOU'RE OUT AND ABOUT on the web, check out some of the sites below. As an alternative to typing in unwieldy internet addresses, I've often thrown in easy-to-remember search terms so you can use Google (or use some other search engine) to find the sites.

These are not definitive lists; they are simply collections of sites that you should visit to get some idea what's available to you. Many have links to other sites related to marketing, advertising, and Baby Boomers, especially the blogs.

Marketing, Mostly

The Boomer Project Matt Thornhill (formerly of Ted Bates and Ogilvy & Mather) and his colleagues are neck-deep in primary Baby Boomer marketing fodder. They are the most dedicated group of professionals I know of in this field. A handful of marketing reports are for sale on the site, but there is plenty of free info, too. *The Boomer Project Newsletter* is another freebie and always a good read.

www.boomerproject.com *or search "Boomer Project"*

The Mature Market This is the best online news source to find Baby Boomer marketing and advertising articles from around the world. Publisher/editor Frederic Serrière oversees online editions from France, Germany, Canada, Belgium, and the U.K. An international edition grabs stories from the other countries. Bookmark it. Each day valuable features, columns, and business-related items are gathered from every news source imaginable.

www.thematuremarket.com *Don't forget to type "the" in the URL. You may be pleasantly surprised or very unpleasantly shocked if you don't. Search "The Mature Market"*

Mary Furlong & Associates Mary has such a varied background in so many disciplines that it's hard to wrap her up in a neat little package. She's a college professor of entrepreneurship, co-founded two major websites (thirdage.com and seniornet.com), has her own company specializing in the 50-plus market, and is deeply involved with projects that bring together major venture capitalists, entrepreneurs, and marketing and advertising professionals. Her annual *What's Next Boomer Summit* and *Boomer Business Challenge* attracts many of the top businesses in the world.

www.maryfurlong.com *or search "Mary Furlong"*

Age Wave Ken and Maddy Dychtwald are seminal thinkers about more than just marketing. Their company defies categorization. I'll just quote something from Age Wave's website:

> Age Wave and *The New York Times* are collaborating on the creation of a timely and unique quarterly advertising series that will be launched in March of 2005 in *The New York Times Magazine* entitled, "The Power Years: A User's Guide to the Rest of Your Life." This first-of-its-kind special series will be devoted to the dynamic, aspirational group of 40-to-60-year-olds who are redefining this new stage of life and will present a positive, prospective approach to adulthood and aging and provide information that enlightens and inspires readers to take action on critical life issues that will benefit themselves, their families and their communities.

www.agewave.com *or search "Age Wave"*

Life Two This is a rambunctious online magazine. Along with original pieces, it does a great job of collecting links to eclectic articles and blogs, and commenting on them.

www.lifetwo.com *or search "Life Two"*

Advertising, Mostly

There isn't much about advertising to Baby Boomers in the U.S. Most of what you will find on the web has an international slant.

SeniorAgency   Jean-Paul Tréguer's agency in France, with international outposts. (Don't tell Jean-Paul I said this, but the Sydney, Australia office has the best website.)

> www.senioragency.com *or search "senior agency"*
> www.senioragencyaustralia.com.au *or search "senioragency Australia"*

J. Walter Thompson Mature Market Group   Yes, a major ad agency has a division focusing on the 45-plus market. It's based in San Francisco. I once joked with someone at JWTMMG, saying that the name should be changed to the J. Walter Thompson *Majority* Market Group, because that's what it really is. No doubt the humor (and truth) would be lost if this were proffered to the powers-that-be in New York and London.

> www.jwtmmg.com *or google "jwt mature market group"*

Brent Green Associates   The author of *Marketing to Leading-Edge Baby Boomers* has an informative PDF for download.

> www.bgassoicates.com *or google "brent green associates"*

Millennium Direct   A mid-sized marketing and advertising agency in England with strategic alliances with a few other companies, including *Evergreen Direct* in Middlebury, Vermont, and *Evergreen Marketing and Communications* in Australia.

> www.millenniumdirect.co.uk/ *or google "millenniumdirect"*
> Evergreen Direct www.evergreendirect.com/
> Evergreen Marketing Communications www.evergreenmc.com.au/

And you can find me by searching "nyrenagency" or "advertising to Baby Boomers"

50 Plus Marketing Based in England, Dick Stroud's company *20plus30* specializes in 50-plus web marketing, but his blog takes on marketing and advertising in all media, in all countries. His entries are always entertaining, biting, and forceful.

A published author of two internet marketing books, Dick also teaches and lectures at various institutions including the Chartered Institute of Marketing and the London Business School.

www.50plus.blogspot.com *or google "stroud marketing blog"*

Ageless Marketing David Wolfe's hopping blog. Mr. Wolfe keeps it current, and always seems to unearth *the* marketing or advertising news story of the day to toss up for comments. A rousing back-and-forth often happens, something rare in most industry blogs. Also on the site are two deep lists: one of recommended books, the other a collection of top-notch marketing blogs.

http://agelessmarketing.typepad.com/ageless_marketing
or search "ageless marketing blog"

The Boomer Report Authors and editors of *After Fifty: How the Baby Boom Will Redefine the Mature Market,* (Paramount Market Publishing, 2003) Howard Willens and Dr. Leslie Harris have fashioned a blog to talk directly to advertisers and marketers. Their book is relatively new, their blog brand new. A link to The Boomer Report blog can be found at:

www.maturemarketing.com

A Handful of Outrageous Advertising Blogs

These are not Baby Boomer specific, but fun to traipse through. Be prepared: Often, there are caustic posts, and if you're not used to such shenanigans, they may startle you. Many people use blogs as a way to blow off steam.

Brand Autopsy I mentioned it in chapter nineteen.

http://brandautopsy.typepad.com *or search "brand autopsy"*

Gaping Void Another favorite advertising sandbox. Hugh Macleod is not a child-safe product. His comments and cartoons are often X-rated. His insights about the advertising industry are triple-A rated.

www.gapingvoid.com *or search "gaping void"*

Adrants Self-explanatory, but you'll also find up-to-date links to relevant news stories about advertising.

www.adrants.com/ *or search "ad rants"*

The companies and individuals above do not come with any specific recommendations from me. I simply want to get you sniffing around so you know that there are many professionals who are very serious about targeting the 50-plus market.

My Blog

http://advertisingtobabyboomers.blogspot.com/

I created a blog around the time the first edition of my book was published. It's taken off (and while my publisher won't like me saying this, in some ways it's become more popular than the book it was designed to promote). The hits are usually deep. People show up and stay there for ten minutes to over an hour. They visit multiple pages. They hit the "print article" button over and over. The domains visiting include large and small ad agencies, consumer product and service companies, colleges and universities, and especially the media. Little bits and pieces of my blog have slipped into newspapers, magazines, marketing books, other web sites—with or without acknowledgments. All fine with me.

And, links to most of the sites mentioned in this chapter are on my blog, along with dozens of others.

Google "Chuck Nyren" or "Advertising to Baby Boomers."

CHAPTER TWENTY-FOUR

Case Study: How a Baby Boomer (Mostly) Company Found Its Market

MACKIE DESIGNS is a good outfit to profile. It has a bit of every-thing for everybody. Founded by an entrepreneurial Baby Boomer, Mackie audio products are sold to both consumers and businesses. The market is narrow, but the age demographics are wide-ranging, with Baby Boomers being the largest group. All advertisers, entrepre-neurs, and marketing professionals can learn something, for the com-pany is not too large and not too small.

Mackie Designs started small in a garage. But twenty years before the garage (and probably in *another* garage), Greg Mackie helped birth a major Baby Boomers cultural revolution.

The Creative Director Speaks

I'll let Ron Koliha tell the Mackie story in his own words, except when I butt in now and then.

First a bit about Ron:

Ron Koliha is a copywriter and creative director whose notable accounts have included Olympia Beer, TDK tape, JVC Electronics, Black Velvet Whiskey, Cuervo Tequila, ITT, *Scientific American,* JBL Speakers, Harman Kardon, and Philips Electronics. Ron started his own ad agency in Seattle after leaving college in the early 1970s. The company handled primarily print and radio. Eventually, Ron sold his agency to NW Ayer (a major agency at the time). In 1978 he moved to New York and worked for Burson-Marsteller, writing copy for JVC consumer electronics and a handful of choice business-to-business accounts.

After a few short-lived jobs and a few crazy life and business adventures, Ron ended up in Los Angeles. "In 1981 I was writing long retail copy for a quirky, locally owned consumer-electronics retail chain. I did it for five years. This turned out to be a unique 'laboratory' for testing copy on a largely Baby Boomer audience. I could write a few hundred words on Wednesday and gauge the sales result on Sunday, modify the pitch and again gauge the change at the end of the week.

"When Greg Mackie started Mackie Designs in 1989, I moved back to Seattle."

Ron and Greg had worked together and had been friends for many years.

A bit about Greg:

"Back in 1968," Ron told me, "when rock bands were forming in almost every garage, Greg noticed that there were no affordable mixers that could handle screaming rock vocalists and loud drums. (Mixers combine all of the various sound sources of a band. microphones, keyboards, and so forth into one signal that is sent to the loudspeakers. It's basically a box with lots of volume and tone controls.)

"What mixers existed were designed for sedate mixing of the spoken word in conference rooms and auditoriums. When a rock musician plugged in a microphone and started shouting over the guitars, the sound was terrible!

"So Greg hunted up some electronic engineers and built the first mixer designed for rock bands. They handled the circuitry; Greg designed the user interface.

"His mixers were a complete success, arriving at a time when there was no competition except the above-mentioned crude or wildly expensive models used by major rock groups like the Rolling Stones. TAPCO (Technical Audio Products Company) grew to sales of $20 million by 1975. At that point it got too big for Greg and he sold out."

I told Ron an anecdote about Greg that I'd heard from an acquaintance. After mentioning Mackie Designs, the person said, "I remember Greg Mackie thirty-five years ago. I was working in a music store and this wild-eyed kid used to come in and hang out. He asked a lot of questions, but didn't buy much. He knew about music, about instruments, but I never got the impression that he was a musician. I wasn't sure what he was after.

"One day he walked in with some sort of contraption with big knobs and wires hanging out every which way, and announced, 'This is a new mixer! It's going to change the music world!'

"And we laughed, and then patted him on the shoulder and said, 'Sure, Greg.'

"A year or two later, the store started selling these relatively inexpensive TAPCO mixers. A few months went by before I realized that this was *Greg's* mixer. We hadn't seen him for awhile. I guess he'd been busy."

Ron chuckled at my recounted story. "Greg Mackie is an intuitive problem solver. Not an engineer, but someone with the talent to perceive a need and then build something that solves the problem. He does this by working with specialized talent such as electronic engineers and then adding an innate ability to design and manufacture easy-to-use products at reasonable prices."

An Affordable, Professional Product

After fifteen years or so, TAPCO mixers were becoming a tad obsolete. So in 1989 Greg was ready to get back into the game. He founded *Mackie Designs*. Along with top-notch engineering and manufacturing crews, Greg hired Ron Koliha as his "advertising department."

Along with improving and updating the basic concept behind the TAPCO mixer, Greg saw another need for inexpensive, professional mixers. "Until the early 1980s," Ron said, "recording your own music well enough to produce a record or CD was an expensive process. You had to purchase time at a recording studio at anywhere from $100 to $500 an hour. Long hours meticulously crafting an album were solely the domain of big popular bands signed to record labels.

"Half of the solution was provided by Greg: an affordable mixer with the features and sound quality required for professional sound. The other half was provided by the introduction of relatively inexpensive digital multi-track recorders. Suddenly, anyone could produce a "quality" album in his or her bedroom. All of the equipment needed cost less than a week of commercial recording studio rental!

"This opened the floodgates of the inspired amateur. It turned out that there were tens of thousands of people who always wanted to produce a commercial (or at least vanity) recording but were stopped by the expense and intimidation of commercial recording studios. Choirs, high school bands, lounge piano players and of course a gazillion rock musicians and bands took advantage of Greg's first *Mackie* mixers."

Getting the Word Out

I asked Ron what his advertising techniques were for Mackie products, especially in the beginning when there wasn't much money to throw around.

"If we had been forced to place our ads in wide-circulation magazines like *Rolling Stone,* our budget wouldn't have gone very far. We were blessed with targeted print media that spoke directly to those who were interested in recording, titles such as *Mix, Recording, Home Recording,* and *Electronic Musician.* You get the idea. So we had an opportunity to directly address an audience that was potentially interested in "a better mousetrap."

"So in this respect the Mackie Designs story is not one of mass marketing. It is the story of introducing a product to a specialized audience, much the same way an ad for a better golf club can be placed in *Golf* magazine, or a better off-road tire ad can be placed in *4-Wheeler* magazine."

Before long, professional audio folks were using *Mackie* mixers. Larger versions were designed and manufactured. By the mid 1990s, Mackie Designs was so successful that it went public. The company began designing and manufacturing other audio products, like speakers and amplifiers.

Why did Mackie Designs Become So Successful?

"The right product at the right time for the right price," Ron said. "Supported by marketing communications that spoke in a distinctive voice and clearly told the reasons why our products were better.

"From the beginning, I made sure that all marketing communications, packaging and even manuals had a warm, friendly, we're-folks-just-like-you tone of voice. If we were just selling to seasoned professional recording engineers, this probably wouldn't have been necessary. But we knew that amateur home recordists needed some assurance that what they bought was easy to use and designed for hobbyists just like they were. So the key was maintaining a 'mixers for dummies' tone while still clearly communicating that our products were of professional quality.

"Other mixer companies continued to project a lofty, haughty image that was intimidating to anyone but a professional engineer. We become the 'Mackoids in the Northwest Rainforest.' People you could relate to instead of a faceless corporation."

Eventually, It Became a Brand

Mackie originally was a product, then a group of products. I asked Ron about his slow, organic branding of *Mackie.*

"There are myriad definitions of 'brand,'" Ron said, "but the one I have always used is 'A brand is a promise you make to the customer.' So building the *Mackie* brand was an exercise in keeping the promise of professional-quality products in affordable, easy-to-use-and-understand packages, made by friendly accessible folks up in Washington State.

"Keeping a promise like that starts, of course, with the product. Mackie products were bulletproof, capable of withstanding coffee spills, drops off the stage, even earthquakes and tornados. Our mixers also performed as promised in terms of high quality sound.

"The next part of the promise was that we were real folks. Our boxes had silly fine print on them to show our sense of humor. The manuals were written in plain, jargon-free English and assumed no experience on the part of the user. We basically explained the whole recording process in each manual, and received an astonishing number of warranty card comments about how fun, informative, and easy-to-read our manuals were.

"On the advertising side, I peopled our ads with Mackie employees, and made sure that Greg Mackie was prominently featured in the ads whenever possible. I wanted the brand to be associated with human beings in a specific location, rather than just a logo. In my mind, this made the branding promise much more realistic; it was a promise from a group of people that the consumer could envision."

Product as Hero

"We never used happy posed models using our equipment. For one thing, our product appealed to too many different sorts of people. Put a 20-something kid in the ad and we risked turning off boomers. Put a Boomer in the ad and turn off younger readers. By cutting directly to the product and building the ad around it, I skipped this problem.

"Frankly, I think too many posed people is a problem in a lot of ads today, and directly applies to boomer marketing. You can't just buy a stock photo CD of 'Active Seniors' or whatever, stick the photos in the ad and call it '*marketing to Boomers*.'"

Which started us talking more about advertising to Baby Boomers and less about Mackie Designs. It's history for Ron, anyway. Greg Mackie sold the bulk of his stock in early 2003, and an investment firm in Florida now controls most of the company.

At the moment, Greg is focusing on two new independent products in development—one aimed at the music industry, another for the general consumer market.

And Ron left Mackie around the same time. He now works freelance, mostly in the audio electronics and home entertainment industry.

"One of the revelations I had a few years ago was a simple bar graph of the population distribution in the U.S. Sure, we all acknowledge that there is a 'bulge' of Baby Boomers. But once you see what it represents quantitatively, it's staggering. This is a GIGANTIC bulge that dwarfs the total population under 30. For all the numeric data agencies swim in, I find it ironic that this one has escaped them. *There are simply more of us.* Or maybe it hasn't escaped them. Maybe it's just easier to chase audiences closer to the age of their creative staff.

"At any rate, by sheer numbers, the *Boomer Bulge* contains more musicians, more persons with well-developed hobbies, and more persons with disposable income.

"A company I currently consult with is marketing a relatively inexpensive, entry level computer recording product. It's a combination of a hardware interface and software that lets you play or sing directly into your computer and then drag the music tracks around with a mouse.

"The client's assumption was that since younger musicians are presumed to be more computer literate and willing to give up the old trappings of mixers and recorders, the product would sell strongly to the 18-to-24 age demographic.

"After six months of fairly brisk sales, somebody got around to checking the warranty cards. It turned out that the median age of a user was 49! Ah, they reasoned, kids don't turn in warranty cards, so this median age is skewed upwards.

"They actually paid for some outside research. Less skew than they thought! The average age of the buyer of this computer music recording system was 48!

"It's not that younger musicians don't record. There are just fewer of them."

CHAPTER TWENTY-FIVE

An Aside For Baby Boomer Creatives*
(in case someone hands you this book)

AS I'VE MENTIONED (probably three or four times too many), I'm not much of a follower, not much into gurus of any sort; I'm a bit jaded, and for sure I'm not a big fan of motivational speakers or authors. You won't find me hanging out in the self-help section of bookstores. Just being anywhere near that aisle gives me the heebie-jeebies.

I am good at writing persuasive copy, creative direction and strategy, and I give pretty good presentation, the latter because I minored in Hammy Acting in college.

All the caveats above are so you know from the get-go that I'm a bit squeamish about what I'm jumping into with this chapter.

I'm going to try to motivate you—to rally the troops. If you are a creative who is a Baby Boomer, those troops would be you.

Marketing folks seem to "get it." With this book, I've tried to persuade people with products for Baby Boomers to "get it." Probably a few got it even before picking up *Advertising to Baby Boomers*. I'm guessing a few more will get it without reading this book. Let's hope so.

The problem is getting advertising agencies to make the big leap. It isn't quite as black and white as I'm making it sound. Yes, some agencies are listening, at least to the "marketing to Baby Boomers" message. However, the second part—actively seeking out Baby Boomer creatives—I don't see that happening, and it won't happen without outside pressure from clients.

Recently I chatted with a marketing consultant friend, someone who is on the road a great deal speaking at conventions, symposiums, and corporate executive gatherings. One of his messages is about targeting the 50-plus market. He told me that he's been burned too many times with this scenario: He convinces someone that it would be wise to market their product or service to Baby Boomers, and the person says, "Let me run it by my advertising agency."

And guess what? The advertising agency dissuades this person.

For a while, when someone said, "Let me run it by . . ." my friend would mention some agencies and freelance professionals who know how to reach the 50-plus market. Of course, the person would run it by his or her agency anyway, and end up dissuaded like all the rest. Now when my friend hears "Let me run it by my . . ." he knows it's a dead end and doesn't do any follow-ups.

How am I doing so far in motivating you?

It gets worse.

A comment I keep hearing is, *"Even when there are advertisements aimed at Baby Boomers, they get it wrong."*

Here are two excerpts from an interview on the website *www. thematuremarket.com* with Matt Thornhill of The Boomer Project:

> Marketers will need to develop new skills in order to craft ✳ messages that will resonate with this segment. This is especially so since so many marketing directors and advertising agency writers and art directors are in their 20s and 30s. Their perception of a 55-year-old is quite different than a 55-year-old's self perception.
>
> —Matt Thornhill

(How about this as a new skill that advertising agencies need to develop: find and recruit Baby Boomer creatives. That'd sort of solve the problem.)

More from the interview:

Question: In your opinion, are American companies ready to adapt their offer to Baby Boomers?

✳ Should we be "promoting" our own age as a "benefit" of CR?

Not yet. But they will. Or they'll shrink. It's that simple. In truth, even if they wanted to adapt their offer to Boomers, they don't know how.

—Matt Thornhill

So let's assume you have, in your hands, comprehensive research provided to you by The Boomer Project (or any number of marketing reports by other firms). What's the obvious next step? How do you apply this research and put these findings into practice?

All together now:

HIRE BABY BOOMER CREATIVES.

I'm sort of getting into this "motivational mode" now. I like it. I'm feeling very much *empowered*. Maybe those self-help books aren't that bad after all. . . .

Okay, so my sarcasm comes from the fact that the answer is *so* obvious, just like the answers in most of those self-help books.

Promote Yourself as a Baby Boomer Creative

But Baby Boomer creatives also have some responsibility: *You must be available.* I mean that in every sense of the word. For example: You must *advertise yourself as a Baby Boomer creative*. I know this will be difficult. I know it when I walk into an ad agency and I'm the oldest person within fifty yards of the cappuccino machine. I know you want to pretend to be twenty years younger. I do that myself, sometimes.

Or, you've given up. Or you do what I do and work freelance. (Which, actually, I like.)

My point is this: If advertising agencies ever get the hint, or are browbeaten by their clients (these would be synonymous), then they'd better have some older creatives to grab fast. This is where a great inspirational speaker would now exclaim, "*You must embrace your . . .* BOOMERNESS!!!"

And there would be wild applause. Followed by some sort of frenzied, mass exhortation, a wild chant or a cheerleading-type yell, over and over. Then a pep rally. Then a march on Madison Avenue, with picket signs. And sit-ins at doctors' offices, where Baby Boomer creatives would stage Botox bottle burnings.

But I'll just say: *Be ready*. Include something in your resume that makes it clear that you are ideal for any campaign where the 40-plus market is part of the mix, or the primary target.

I'd do it all myself, but with a trillion dollars of billing each year over the next twenty-five years, well, my old Burroughs manual adding machine doesn't have that many zeros.

CHAPTER TWENTY-SIX

The Revolution

MY GUESS IS that the revolution will be a quiet one, and that it will happen within the next two or three years. It won't be high profile, and most likely you may not hear about it until it's over. Here's what will happen.

The Prediction: A Baby Boomer at the helm of a small or medium-sized agency will roll up his or her sleeves, get his or her hands dirty with copy and design (or hire a few of his or her creative buddies from the old days), and fashion a campaign for a general consumer product, with Baby Boomers as the target market.

The ethos will be there. The aesthetics will be there. The humor will be there. A more mature sense of purpose will be there. And the customers will be there—millions of them. That's just one possible scenario. Who knows how it will really happen. But it will.

What Wasn't Included in This Book and Why

Oodles of Marketing Fodder: You can find that everywhere, books, articles, and online. A number of marketing firms offer detailed reports on the 50-plus market. I tried to focus on advertising. However, the disciplines often bleed into one another.

Baby Boomer Cohorts: Again, this is within the marketing sphere—and there's a ton of information out there. Baby Boomers are not an amorphous bunch, all with the same values, living the same lives, but a zeitgeist is shared. The main Baby Boomer cohorts for me are:

1. Women and Men

2. Leading-Edge and Late (or Trailing-Edge) Boomers

3. Ethnic and Cultural

4. Economic and Cultural

But I don't even consider the above cohorts to be set in stone, or always relevant. You can spend the better part of your life coming up with Baby Boomer cohorts, until you've finally found 76 million cohorts. Then you'll be trying to sell one product to one person at a time.

> I notice increasing reluctance on the part of marketing executives to use judgment; they are coming to rely too much on research, and they use it as a drunkard uses a lamp post for support, rather than for illumination.
> —David Ogilvy[1]

Whoops. Looks like I've just alienated every marketing professional in the world with the above quote.

But Mr. Ogilvy also said this:

> Advertising people who ignore research are as dangerous as generals who ignore decodes of enemy signals.
> —David Ogilvy[2]

A contradiction? No, just putting things in perspective.

Leave the numbers and research with the Creatives. Then leave them alone. If you have people working on the campaign who are within the age range and the cultural boundaries of your target market(s), your product will be in good hands.

If the product is for Baby Boomer women, find a Baby Boomer woman creative director, copywriter, graphic artist, or photographer. There are thousands out there, some with their own agencies. *Don't trust the soul of the campaign to anybody else,* including me. Meaning, if I were the creative director for a product targeting

---

1 David Ogilvy, *Confessions of an Advertising Man* (New York: Ballantine Books, 1971).

2 David Ogilvy, *Ogilvy on Advertising* (New York: Crown Publishers, 1983)

Baby Boomer women, I would insist on at least two Baby Boomer women as part of the team. (And while I'd be the boss, I'd defer to their judgment.)

Use this as a guide for a few of the other cohorts I've mentioned. Mix and match. Demand the right people for the right jobs, or at least one or two of the right people for one or two of the jobs. *They need to be there.*

At some point, a good advertising creative stops analyzing the research, blows the marketing dust out of his or her head (leaving a thick coat of residue on the inner wall of the brain cavity), and creates a campaign.

For an advertising creative, research will illuminate, but it won't inspire.

How to Create a Marketing and Advertising Campaign for Baby Boomers from Start to Finish: This is painting-by-numbers stuff. I'd stay away from anything that smacks of "how-to." As an advertiser or client, you don't need to know that much about it. However, you do need to know about and put into practice much of what is in this book. It's *your* product or service that is being advertised. Don't roll over for any advertising agency. Insist on some fundamentals and then let them do their jobs.

How to Be a Baby Boomer Advertising Creative: Another paint-by-numbers scam. Sure, creatives will get something out of flipping though this book. They will pick up a few things they hadn't thought of, and whatever they grab will probably be used as catalysts for even better ideas.

I've laid down a few rules and regulations, and set up a playing field. But nothing would make me happier than if some Baby Boomer creatives put together a campaign, ended up breaking all my rules, and hit a home run out of the stadium.

I trust Baby Boomer creatives. So should you.

And I've learned much from other Baby Boomer creatives and GenX and GenY creatives, and now a few Echo Boomer creatives, and way before all of them, from the giants of advertising over the last one hundred years.

And That Is the Point of This Book

Each re-invention of advertising has had its blind spots. More often than not, these blind spots had to do with diversity.

Circling back to the beginning of this book:

Up until the beginning of the last century, advertising was simply an extension of sales. When advertising became big business, Ivy Leaguers took over. It was thought that only Eastern, college-educated grads could write advertising copy and create campaigns. With the emergence of mass media, advertising had to reach a wider demographic. Advertising wasn't so hoity-toity anymore. The industry diversified.

Age was never much of a factor. Agencies were full of old, middle-aged, and young people. When more complex demographics were thrown into the mix, advertising agencies looked to women and minorities to add to their creative stables. But all these new demographics had one thing in common: *youth.* By the mid-Seventies, twenty-year-olds and thirty-year-olds had taken over ad agencies. Now, age demographics are as important as all other demographics.

It's time for another change; time for diversity. Advertising agencies need to add Baby Boomers to the mix. They need a healthy blend of professionals of all ages.

I could lock myself in my office for a year and study marketing and research reports about target markets aged 19-to-30 day and night, watch MTV and the WB Network until my eyeballs burned their sockets, slip out every so often and "hit the streets," but I'll never be able to put together an ad campaign targeting twenty-year-olds better than an advertising professional in his or her twenties. I might come close, but chances are I'd miss the mark.

There is one, possibly two, genius advertising creatives in their forties, fifties or even in their sixties who probably could reach the twenty-something demographic. There is one, possibly two, genius advertising creatives in their twenties who could probably reach the forty-to-sixty age demographic.

But I don't know who or where they are.

AFTERWORD TO THE SECOND EDITION

Recently I have been embarrassed to be part of this generation. The reason? Madison Avenue. Madison Avenue is never
wrong. They're the neighbor across the street that sees you in
the way you don't see yourself. They're young, they're cocky,
and what they say about the older generation becomes the
truth. People still think there was a real Mr. Whipple, so I know
whatever Madison Avenue says about us is what everyone's
going to believe anyway.

—Albert Brooks[1]

MUCH HAS HAPPENED since the first edition of *Advertising to Baby
Boomers* was published. Advertisers, marketers, agencies—even the
media—have acknowledged the existence of a 50+ market. They're
still not sure what to do with it, but know they should be doing
something.

The quotes I've extracted for this chapter were all written (or spoken) since the first edition was written. What they show is that most
advertising still isn't effective. In fact, much of it is counterproductive.
Instead of using the sensibilities required for reaching this diverse market, ad agencies are taking the easy way out by trying to sell their target market *to* their target market. Baby Boomers know who they are,
and where they are in their lives. They don't need or appreciate blatant, ham-fisted pandering.

Nearly one-quarter of U.S. baby-boomers are insulted by the
advertising messages that companies are sending them, accord-

---

1 Albert Brooks, "Boomer Files," *Newsweek*, November 14, 2005

ing to a new study. . . . The survey suggested that many companies were taking a misguided approach as they attempted to reach out to the largest and wealthiest group of U.S. consumers.

—Joshua Chaffin, *The Financial Times*[2]

Trusting Your Gut

In November 2006, *Advertising Age* and *Creativity Magazine* sponsored an Idea Conference in New York City. One speaker was David Jones, Global Chief Executive Officer of Euro RSCG Worldwide.

Taking a "swipe at the research and pre-testing industry," Mr. Jones next exhorted listeners to stop asking permission. Drawing on a "truth" from British comedian Vic Reeves that "96.2% percent of all statistics are made up," Mr. Jones, also a Brit, argued that some of the most well-liked ads aren't based on research or focus-group results. Instead, they rely on a creative director's gut instinct of what consumers will like. He cited Procter & Gamble's effort for Charmin toilet tissue created by Euro rival Publicis Worldwide that riffs off of the many euphemisms for elimination. "Publicis took a risk, and did it without a bit of research," he said.

And by way of reinforcing the previous point, his last bit of advice was for creatives to "trust your gut." Advertising is changing fast, and to not take a risk is risky—even though it's scary to take a risk.[3]

No argument from me. I love it. But there is one big problem. When fashioning campaigns for Baby Boomers, you have to have the right guts around to trust. That'd be 45+ creative guts. Even 60+ creative guts.

It wouldn't be very smart to trust *my* gut to come up with a campaign for a product aimed at twentysomethings. My gut would tell me, *"Ummm . . . ummm . . . Wait! I got it! We get some twentysomething an' spike her hair an' give her tattoos an' a nose ring an' put an iPod on her head playin' an' bed some hip-hop music an' have her hold up the toothpaste! Yeah! They'll buy it! They'll buy it!"*

2 Joshua Chaffin, "Ads Sent Wrong Message," *The Financial Times* and MSNBC, September 4, 2006
3 Lisa Sanders, "Ignore the Research and Trust Your Gut," *Advertising Age*, November 2, 2006

Sixties music. Peace signs. They'll buy it. Portraying Boomers as teenagers with gray hair. They'll buy it.

Actually, I'm talking (again) about diversity and playing the odds.

> "The advertising industry is notoriously associated with young people, crazy ideas, wild parties, and general excessiveness. The average age in the industry is way below thirty. . . . Advertising agencies are in the business of creativity. They are also in the business of managing human perceptions. It's therefore interesting that although many tactics are employed to ensure creativity, agencies have traditionally not cottoned on to the fact that a more diverse workforce, inclusive of non-discriminatory age policies, poses the potential for greater competitive advantage."
>
> —Paula Sartini, *MarketingWeb.com*[4]

David Jones advises the ad industry to take risks with their creative. I agree. The irony is that advertisers and ad agencies have no problem taking the dumbest of risks already: they trust their twenty- and thirtysomething creatives to possess the sensibilities required to reach a demographic beyond their ken.

Nostalgia: It's Over

> You hear The Who's "Happy Jack" followed by "I Can See for Miles." It sounds like a commercial for *The Who's Greatest Hits,* but it's Hummer and a headlight manufacturer hawking their products . . . if this keeps up, maybe there's a *The Who's Greatest Commercial Hits* down the road.
>
> —Bob Baird, *Gannett News Service*[5]

Financial planning companies are all agog over Baby Boomers. Without mentioning names, a handful have gone the nostalgia route. Why they've done this is beyond me. If anything smacks of the future and not the past, it's financial planning. It's also the easy route. No thinking involved. Not much creativity, either.

---

4 Paula Sartini, "Managing Age Diversity in the Advertising Industry," *MarketingWeb.com,* September 4, 2006

5 Bob Baird, *The Journal News,* Gannett Co., June 2005

But the egregiousness of nostalgia in advertising is, again, the *pandering*. And most folks in their fifties and sixties catch on fast. I blogged about this in April 2005. Before long the press and other blogs were all over it:

> "In-A-Gadda-Da-Vida" is being used to get aging hippies to invest for retirement. It's in a (*financial planning company*) commercial. Define irony. I strongly doubt that when a circle of stoned 19-year-olds were passing around a joint with Iron Butterfly on the turntable in 1969, they were weighing wealth-preservation versus growth as they considered the most prudent mix of stocks, bonds and other equity instruments. . . . I find that a bit patronizing. That's how you talk to old people who are, like, I don't know, over 50 or something."
> —Mark Patinkin, *The Providence Journal*[6]

> The 1960s were about cultural change and political activism. But in ———'s new commercials, the era's touchstones are evoked in the name of money, money, money.
> —Patrick Somerville, *The Simon*[7]

> Hope I get a tax-deferred variable annuity before I grow old.
> —Karen Heller, *The Philadelphia Inquirer*[8]

> Iron Butterfly's in an IRA ad? Bummer.
> —Michael Stetz, *San Diego Union-Tribune*[9]

> "In-A-Gadda-Da-What?" They go too far. Just when I got used to hearing our music used as pseudo-symbolic themes, marketing everything from cars to box stores, along comes ———, who are shameless enough to use "In-A-Gadda-Da-Vida" to convince us to hand over our money. At least the other brazen carpetbaggers pretend to try to tie the song into the product."
> —*Aging Hipsters* blog[10]

6　Mark Patinkin, "A '60s Anthem is Sold as Bait," *Providence Journal*, March 2006
7　Patrick Somerville, "Woodstock, Flower Power and Mutual Funds," *The Simon magazine*, March 30, 2006
8　Karen Heller, "Aging, the Boomer Way," *The Philadelphia Inquirer*, March 19, 2006
9　Michael Stetz, "Iron Butterfly's in an IRA ad? Bummer." *San Diego Union-Tribune*, April 2, 2006
10　http://theaginghipster.blogspot.com/

Tonight I alerted my dad to this commercial (he was born in '53) and he sighed with exasperation.

—a comment on my blog

How does a company get snookered into buying into such claptrap? The answer is that it all starts with flawed research, the results of which are almost certainly memorialized by whip smart under-40 creatives (or immature over-40 creatives) who have total certainty about their ability to speak "boomerese."

—Ageless Marketing blog[11]

This is what I can't figure out: What Baby Boomer cohort are they are targeting? Ad agencies seem to have no idea what "The Sixties" meant to any of us. Liberal, cultural progressives took the decade very seriously. They don't enjoy seeing it trivialized, commercialized, reduced to hawking products and services. Conservative Baby Boomers never bought into The Sixties' culture and ethos. Using it thematically to reach them insults and angers them. Then there is a chunk of Boomers who were never particularly affected by it all, shied away from it, had quieter values. Another huge chunk were too young for Sixties Culture to really resonate with them. So what cohort is it? Must be one I don't know about.

Purely anecdotal: I'm watching TV. I hear a tune I haven't heard in thirty-five, or forty years. My mind goes off into the ether. *"Wow. What a great song. I'd forgotten all about it. I had the album. The cover was blue . . . And there were a bunch of other great songs on that album. What the hell were they? I can't remember . . . I wonder if I can get* *** If you must know,** *it on Amazon. There's probably only a compilation of his hits,* **it was Donovan's** *or a boxed set. But I just want the CD of the album. I'll have* **"Catch the Wind."** *to remember to check the next time I'm online . . ."**

By then, the commercial is over. In fact, probably three other commercials are over. I have no idea what the product is, or what any of the the other products are.

I predict that there is going to be a backlash against advertisers that pander to boomers soon. Too many nostalgic songs,

---

11 http://agelessmarketing.typepad.com/

too many advertisements showing boomers smiling and "living life to the fullest." We're savvy, we're complicated.
    —Karen Orton-Katz, boomer marketing consultant

Nostalgia. It's over.

Information vs. Emotion

In chapter eleven I tossed together a tongue-in-cheek scenario of me strolling up and down a toothpaste aisle and not knowing what to buy because I had no idea what product would be best for someone my age. I also mentioned that one way of "cutting through the clutter" would be to come up with a plainer package, or at least one that didn't look like a space-age Christmas tree ornament.

That chapter was written over two years ago. Now, we have a product and campaign that matches my imagination. While the company and agency might not admit it, the primary target market is Boomers:

> In a bid to regain the sales lead from its rival Colgate-Palmolive, the Procter & Gamble Company has introduced Crest Pro-Health, which claims to deliver in one tube everything a consumer could possibly want in a toothpaste. . . . New advertising for Crest Pro-Health will feature real people who have tried and liked the product. "We've gotten an unprecedented amount of testimonials from consumers."
> —Louise Kramer, *New York Times*[12]

Information vs. Emotion and a slew of variants have been argued about since the beginning of modern advertising. At first glance, it's obvious that the print ad for Crest Pro-Health is merely informational. The layout and copy are simple and direct, with two columns of boxes (gingivitis, plaque, cavities, sensitivity, whiteness, and so forth), which compare "an ordinary toothpaste" to Crest Pro-Health. Of course, Crest has all the boxes checked, the "ordinary toothpaste" only a few. Not surprisingly, the television spots are likewise simple and direct.

12 Louise Kramer, "In a Battle of Toothpastes, It's Information vs. Emotion ," *New York Times*, January 17, 2007

You might say, "What a ho-hum, dumb campaign." Yet:

Crest Pro-Health Toothpaste Launch Has P&G Smiling

Three months after its debut, Crest Pro-Health could be the most successful U.S. toothpaste launch in the last decade.... The study found two-thirds of Pro-Health buyers normally use other non-Crest brands of toothpaste, including nearly 25% who said they used Colgate Total, Crest's main rival . . . Pro-Health's secret? Targeting the needs of consumers who put a premium on the healthcare aspects of their toothpaste.... Morgan Stanley expects Pro-Health's sales to increase further. The report noted that "those who had seen Pro-Health ads were 40–50% more likely to buy it."

—*Brandweek*[13]

And it looks like someone must've also read chapter twenty where I talked about over-the-top, empty branding silliness:

In many instances, buyers perceive little difference among such products, so ads often try to entertain consumers or play up brand image while playing down actual attributes. In this case, Procter and Colgate-Palmolive seek to persuade consumers that there are significant distinctions between their toothpastes that could potentially affect health.

—*New York Times*[14]

Sounds like an old fashioned, *Unique Selling Proposition* to me. There are two fascinating things you should know about the Crest Pro-Health campaign. First, this is a strange approach for the agency involved. It's the same agency I mentioned earlier, the one that espouses creating "love" for a new product even though there is no reason on earth to love something you've never used. Second, oddly enough, it *does* elicit an emotional response from Baby Boomers. Why? Because it's a throwback to campaigns we grew up with. It's not heavy-handed, insulting nostalgia, not cheesy graphic retro, but it does use the same USP techniques as many advertisements in the 1950s and early 1960s.

13 Constantine von Hoffman, "Crest Pro-Health Toothpaste Launch Has P&G Smiling," *Brandweek*, October 23, 2006
14 Louise Kramer, "In a Battle of Toothpastes, It's Information vs. Emotion ," *New York Times*, January 17, 2007

We rarely see this anymore, at least with major campaigns.

Will this fact-based approach work with all products and services for Baby Boomers? Of course not. But we're talking toothpaste here.

This same agency knows what to do with Pillsbury and Cheerios. That's what they're good at. So good for them to toss their "love" philosophy out the window for Crest Pro-Health. It's brave. And smart.

Gimme Some Lovin'

There is this advertising philosophy that has to do with "product love." It works fine with products already loved, like Cheerios or "somethin' from the oven." Over time, a brand may become loved. Slowly and with caution, this should be reflected in the advertising.

But loving a product or service you've never used or experienced before? Loving a financial advisor? You might end up loving a financial advisor in five or ten years—or you might hate him (or her). Who knows?

This Is How We Do It

Many pages ago I talked about commercials and infomercials—doing something creative but real (no storyboarding), along with hiring Baby Boomer directors, writers, producers. Let me use that chapter as a basis for a pretend "pitch."

The client is a medium-sized financial planning company. It has a mix of their its own financial advisors (FAs) and independent FAs. The company's offerings are part cookie-cutter, part hands-on planning. I would:

- Find out which of the FAs are the friendliest, the most personable, the sharpest.

- Spend time on the phone talking to these FAs, asking them this or that—not necessarily questions related to their work. What I'm really looking for are ones who make strangers feel comfortable and secure.

- Personally visit or screen the top ten—and pick three or four for the campaign.

- Ask the FAs for "before and after" portfolios of their clients (names blocked out for confidentiality). I'm more interested in the before portfolios. With their help, we would come up with a handful of typical, generic portfolios.

- Hire unknown, professional actors who are comfortable improvising. I might toss in a few non-professionals to mix it up.

- Give them the prepared portfolios to study.

- Hire a top-notch veteran director, a top-notch cinematographer. Two or three cameras.

- Without much more preparation, toss an FA and two actors into an office. (Sure—there is much more to this, but you get the idea.)

- Repeat this scenario several times with different principals.

- Hire a veteran editor.

These cinema-vérité influenced pieces are the type Baby Boomers grew up with. I'd eschew jiggly camerawork. Think less style and more substance. No specific plans or advice mentioned (obviously). Real dialogue, real reactions, real interactions. As close as you can get to a real story, expertly told by the director, the cinematographer, the editor: This is what happens when you visit one of our financial planners. **This is how we do it.**

I would want Baby Boomers watching the spots to simply say to themselves, "That's what *I* need to do. And it doesn't look frightening. Or difficult. Or mind-numbing."

No high-concept branding silliness. No empty, aspirational gobbledygook. No scare tactics. Your financial advisor is not a loveable rock star, the Pillsbury Doughboy, or the harbinger of homelessness.

A boring spot? Not likely with the right creatives. Is there a chance of an ad agency pitching this idea to a client? None. It can't be storyboarded and advertisers and agencies are too afraid to take a chance with creative.

But if it were produced. . . . A Clio? Not a chance. Return on Investment? A really good chance.

Watching Television Commercials

> It's a funny game, advertising. Few want to get serious about
> targeting those with the money—the older age brackets—
> which gives the network with the young guns a handy posi-
> tion. But it will change when the advertising herd does start a
> meaningful migration to older folks.
>
> —Paul McIntyre[15]

Financial companies know that many of us could and should use
financial planning. Drug companies know we use prescription drugs.
If you're a woman, one or two cosmetic firms know that you might
want make-up. And apparently we like to eat mushy, warm biscuits
sold to us in small, expensive packages. But that's about it.

Watching television commercials, you'd think that I haven't
brushed my teeth, bought laundry soap, or taken a shower in almost
twenty years. And as far as big-ticket items—well, those rabbit ears
work just fine on my 13-inch black and white TV. They just require
a nudge and a jiggle every now and then, that's all. And if I need a
new needle for my phonograph, I just get in my '73 Pinto and head
over to the Goodwill and, when no one's looking, twist one off a
dusty old turntable and wedge it in the front pocket of my 30-year-
old chinos.

As I write this, a new campaign for a men's clothing company is
making waves. In a *Wall Street Journal* article, the CMO says they have
dumped their youth-marketing strategy and are now targeting Baby
Boomers in their fifties and sixties.

But something's very strange. As I watch the ads, they feature a
pair of fortysomething bullies. These very unhip guys throw a daugh-
ter's boyfriends out a window, destroy a teenager's car sound system,
hassle a wimpy guy walking his dog, and humiliate a teenage son by
flinging a wet sponge at him.

It sounds like I don't like these commercials—but I don't mind
them. I chuckled. I admire commercials that take chances, cause trou-

---

15 Paul McIntyre, "Younger Audience Near Its Use-by Date," *Sydney Morning Herald,* September 22,
    2005

ble. The problem is that *the campaign has nothing to do with Baby Boomers.* The spots are funny, sort of outrageous, cute, unfortunately a bit patronizing—and won't resonate with most men over forty-five. That's because they have that *Married with Children/King of the Hill* lowest common denominator feel. While I got a big kick out of *Married with Children*, I don't remember ever wanting to wear Al Bundy's clothes.

Add to this the Boomer grandparent ethos. Not too many are still parents of teenagers, or have antipathy towards children and teenagers today. If anything, they are doing everything in their power to *befriend and influence Millennials*—especially their grandchildren.

> Of the 78 million grandparents in the United States, 39 million are Baby Boomer grandparents—and thousands more swell the ranks daily.
> —Press Release for *GRAND* Magazine

> Boomers think their grandkids are too programmed, and they're looking to stir things up.
> —David Kaplan, *The Houston Chronicle*[16]

Does this agency really want to make a truly outrageous, socially irresponsible, slaphappy spots that would resonate with Baby Boomers? How about a scenario where a couple of overbearing parents are telling their two kids what to think, what to do—silly, pointless, manipulative advice—then have a youngish Boomer grandfather and his friend throw *the parents* out the window, to the delight of their grandchildren. Have the Baby Boomer grandparent *help* his grandkid install a loud sound system in his car, to the horror of the kid's parents.

If this clothing company wants to reach the average, middle-aged, angry white guy, then this is a great campaign. If the company wants to reach Baby Boomers, it needs to do a bit of research.

Or perhaps the company and/or its ad agency are simply paying lip service to the idea of a 50+ market, and never really planned on targeting Baby Boomers in the first place.

---

16 David Kaplan, "Grand-scale Grandparents," *Houston Chronicle*, November 2006

The Media

In March, 2006 I hosted a table at the Authors' Luncheon at the Mary Furlong/ASA/BFA *What's Next?* Boomer Business Summit in Anaheim. A gentleman sitting next to me (he didn't actually push and shove people out of the way to do so—but did want to make sure he had a seat at my table) was the Senior V.P. of Research for Nick@Nite and TV Land. We chatted throughout lunch. He'd read my book, said he'd given a few copies to the sales staff.

A month later, this came out:

TV LAND Suggests Ignoring Boomers is Billion-Dollar Mistake

The Nielsen Media Research demos that media buyers and marketers use to bet billions of TV dollars aren't in line with market forces, well-known demographer Ken Dychtwald told a roomful of media buyers and marketers. . . . Instead of the in-demand demo of 18- to 34-year-olds, marketers should target the 40-to-60 set. According to network executives, about 70% of its audience is within the boomer demo. . . . "We've done focus groups with this demo who say they turn on the TV and there are 500 channels and they can't find anything to watch," he said. "They start to feel annoyed, like media has blatantly disregarded them."9

        —Abbey Klaassen, *Advertising Age*[17]

A dozen or so articles and reports were released soon after. It certainly seemed obvious that the television industry would be getting the message. I assumed they had and . . . well, part of my book would become obsolete. Obsolete, but at least the message is being heard loud and clear. Let's consider it successful obsolescence.

Then in November 2006 I read this:

The *Wall Street Journal* recently published a noteworthy error in an article about NBC's *Studio 60 on the Sunset Strip*, stating that the modestly-rated show was attracting about 4 million

---

17 Abbey Klaassen, *Advertising Age*, April 2006

viewers—half as many as its lead-in, the surprise hit *Heroes*. One problem: *Studio 60* has been drawing just under 8 million viewers lately, and *Heroes* well over 14 million. As for the millions watching who were inadvertently erased, their crime is that they don't happen to fall within the 18-to-49 age bracket employed to negotiate advertising rates. Sure, it was a simple omission, but one fraught with symbolism. After all, the industry regularly disenfranchises an older audience whose patronage can't readily be sold to media buyers . . .

—Brian Lowry, *Variety*[18]

Media buyers. Well, they're not really the sole reason for all this marketing myopia. But they play their part.

Back when I was anchoring the syndicated business program *Banmiller on Business*, my boss Kevin O'Brien dragged me to New York to help "sell the show" to ad agencies. To my surprise, we made "pitches" not in boardrooms, but in backrooms. O'Brien, a seasoned salesman, walked me though the corridors that connected cubicles housed with [*sic*] people in their 20s, who were actually making the buying decisions for their clients. O'Brien knew them all by first names. And not surprisingly, they were buying shows they watched. When I suggested we were not talking to "the right people," he just smiled. He knew how the system worked. I did not.

—Brian Banmiller[19]

Should we blame only those young media buyers?

Those who run the firms that buy the ads, Baby Boomers in their fifties, are in denial, said Mike Irwin, president and CEO of Focalyst. . . . "It is especially hard to convince execs of the need to focus on the 50-plus market, even though most of them are 50-plus themselves.

—Ruth Solomon, Sun-Times News Group[20]

18 Brian Lowry, "Demographic Static: Older folks just don't matter anymore to the TV biz," *Variety*, November 14, 2006

19 Brian Banmiller, "Anchors Away from Age Bias, *San Francisco Chronicle*, June 11, 2006

20 Ruth Solomon, "Marketing to Boomers," *Sun-Times* News Group, November 2, 2006

Mr. Banmiller also informs us about the magazine industry:

I've since had this reality check confirmed by two magazine marketing executives who are major players in the New York publishing scene. Apparently it also happens in print. Over a long dinner, they expressed the same frustration. They . . . wonder why there is such a focus on younger (and poorer) readers.

—Brian Banmiller[21]

A comment left on my blog from the publisher of a magazine targeting Baby Boomers shared his frustrations with media buyers:

Chuck,

We are experiencing just about every stereotypical reaction from 20-something agency media buyers you can imagine. With a few notable agency—side exceptions, our success to date—and there's still a long way for us to go—has been finding Boomer athletes in the marketing departments at clients who then direct the agency to deal with us. Or better yet, we've found a couple of forward-thinking advertisers— Michelob Ultra and 3M come to mind—who handle their media buying in-house and are aggressively targeting the active Boomer market . . .

—Brian Reilly, publisher, *GeezerJock Magazine*

The average media buyer or planner is under 30. Many are undoubtedly hired for their know-how in appealing to a specific generation, and it isn't the baby boomers.

—David Bauder, *AP News*[22]

And the inexcusable irony is this: Of all the age demo groups, Baby Boomers are the *easiest to reach*. They watch the most television, are the largest age group listening to (great retronym) *terrestrial* radio, they're the ones reading magazines and newspapers, are all over the

---

Web, and spend the most money attending live events. It's hard *not* to reach them.

And yet ...

> To a surprising extent, advertising is also alienating. The Harris Interactive study found that half of baby boomers say they tune out commercials that are clearly aimed at young people. An additional one-third said they'd go out of their way NOT to buy such a product.
>
> —David Bauder[23]

I could say that all this is short-sighted, stupid, a disservice to advertisers, and perhaps a disservice to consumers. But what I really think is this: it's surreal. Eerie. Tens of millions of people over age forty-five are reading, listening, watching, and absorbing mass media. Advertising messages are placed where and when they should be—but they are not seen, not heard. Or they are subconsciously batted away.

And the bureaucrats likewise ignore it all. It's Kafkaesque.

The Web and Technology

The worldwide web isn't doing much better. Mostly this is due to misconceptions about Baby Boomers and our knowledge of technology. We're lumbering Luddites, according to conventional wisdom.

Mozilla, the non-profit company with it's upstart browser Firefox, certainly thinks so:.

> "There are more than 63 million baby boomers and 25 million senior citizens online, and Mozilla figures the best way to reach them is for their more tech-savvy kids or relatives to install Firefox for them."
>
> —*Businessweek*[24]

But research (and common sense) tells a different story:

Forrester Research also found that very few online travelers

23 Ibid.
24 Sarah Lacy, "Mozilla Goes Mainstream," *Businessweek*, August 20, 2006

start searches using the new breed of travel search engines—most likely because they are not aware of their existence . . . Hitwise found that visitors to the top travel search engines were by far likely to be over 55 years of age. Hitwise attributed this to baby boomers.

—Jeffrey Grau, iMedia Connection[25]

A new U.S. survey has shown that it's not young people who are driving the growth in podcasting, but the older generation. A survey of over 8,000 American consumers by pollsters CLX has revealed that podcasting is most popular with those over 45, with 21 percent of those questioned listening to podcasts. This compares to just 13 percent of 15-to-24-year olds.

—*What PC?* [26]

Three of five adults aged 55 years and older, known to be the heaviest consumers of offline media such as newspapers and TV network news, say they use the Internet more today than they did a year ago. This data is supported by comScore Media Metrix research, which finds the number of online adults aged 55 and older grew by 20 percent to reach over 27 million in 2005. . . . This age group also finds more accurate information on the Web than with TV, radio, magazines, and newspapers.

—Tessa Wegert, ClickZ Network[27]

Ms. Wegert goes on to tell a funny story about her parents-in-law showing up at an extended-family Christmas gathering with webcams for everybody:

The "kids"—all of us in our late 20s and early 30s—stared at each other in disbelief. The mood in the room was one of pride mingled with private inadequacy. As they boast the latest in

25 Jeffrey Grau, "How Consumers Use Online for Travel," imediaconnection.com, November 11, 2005

26 Iain Thomson, "Youth of Today Spurn Podcasting," *What PC?,* August 19, 2005

27 "Baby Boomers Burst Online," ClickZ Network, January 5, 2006

28 Ibid.

computer technology, including iPods, navigation systems, and Apple's PowerMac G5, my 50-something parents-in-law are on top of the trends. . . . "Now we can all iChat together and see each other wherever we are," she told us. "Later, I'll show you all how to set it up."

—Tessa Wegert[28]

The computer/internet ethos for most Baby Boomers is that they pick and choose what technology they want to use, buy, or install. Some are all over Skype, video and music uploading and download-ing, research, education, travel planning, shopping—while eschewing blogging, communities, and web page design. Or it's the other way around. Or variations thereof. When it comes to new technology, most Baby Boomers learn only about what interests them, what they believe will be useful. They don't feel the need to know everything there is to know about technology, computers, and the web.

And Firefox? I use Firefox. I admire Mozilla's philosophy. No doubt lots of Baby Boomers would identify with and champion a bunch of rebellious folk who question authority and the status quo, that and who created a product out of love and not for profit. We've always liked idealistic troublemakers. In fact, I might be willing to join in and do a bit of free Firefox evangelizing—maybe by writing some copy explaining in down-to-earth language the advantages of Fire-fox. Something in a style that Baby Boomers would find appealing and relevant.

But sadly, because I'm over fifty, I'm too much of a technological imbecile to figure out how to find Mozilla on the web and email them. I'll have to wait until some "tech-savvy kid" comes over so he or she can do it for me.

Webs Sites for Baby Boomers

Web pundits are drooling over social networking sites. While this busi-ness model is successful and will continue to be, I'm not convinced that people over fifty really care about *la-de-da* virtual socializing. There has to be a reason to join and hang out other than simply being a Baby Boomer. Sites that center around specific interests like gardening, politics, health, travel, dating, food, art, sports, real estate, education, grandparenting, volunteering, mentoring, etc. will attract a 50+ base. But few want or need to simply hop online and proclaim, "Hello! I'm Joe and I'm a Baby Boomer!"

What will separate the winners and losers? Compelling, deep, entertaining, vital content. Here are two projects to I'd keep keep an eye on:

The Active Living Network This is the brainchild of Marc Middleton, a former TV news anchor and producer in Orlando, Florida. Marc taught himself a few web development and design programs and in 2005 launched GrowingBolder.com. His company also produces informational and entertaining human interest videos, along with a syndicated radio program.

A few backers and advertisers are paying attention. In early 2007 the site will be completely redesigned. All elements will be seamlessly woven into quite an exciting site. Be prepared for video and audio podcasts, timely articles, and all sorts of fun, engaging, educational features. Mr. Middleton understands that content will bring them in and keep them coming back.

Wobo Media Inc. Mindy Herman was president and CEO of E! Networks for five years. She's now president of Wobo Media Inc., a company that will target Baby Boomers.

Wobo's initial product launch will be a state-of-the-art web site . . . with a rich array of originally-produced broadband video and rich media informational and lifestyle content. Wobo will combine both its own production capability with the ability for its users to learn to produce and share their own content in areas such as health, fitness, well-being, finance, fashion, career, etc.[29]

Mytime.com it's called. My guess is that with Ms. Herman's background, it won't be boring.

---

[29] Online notes for the Wharton Technology Conference, 2006

Most sites hoping to attract Baby Boomers *are* boring. They have very little real content—or much of anything. What is there is usually generic advice and bland aphorisms. Quoting Gertrude Stein, "There is no *there* there."[30]

Marc Middleton and Mindy Herman may change all that.

Word of Mouth: A Tool in Your Arsenal

In August, 2005 I left some posts on the John Moore's *Brand Autopsy* blog (http://brandautopsy.typepad.com/).The thread was about word-of-mouth marketing (WOMM). Here are a few snippets:

> I'm not anti-WOM. I know it's been effective within certain demographics and for certain products. But it's nothing new. The marketing channels are new, the way WOM travels (and originates) is new.
>
> But there isn't a magic WOM wand. For the last fifteen years or so, people have been passing themselves off as "branding experts' with magic branding wands. Branding *vs.* Advertising. Eventually, advertisers caught on that branding is simply a weapon in a large arsenal of ways to reach and keep consumers—not the be all and end all.

Now the WOM people are waving their wands. In a few years there will be a new blog: *WOM Autopsy.*

> Branding and WOM and good copywriting and design and TV and radio spots and long-form commercials for cable and the internet and print ads and PR and everything else will still all be weapons in all marketing and advertising arsenals.
>
> WOM needs to be WOMed and put into practice in many (but probably not all) campaigns. It should be taken seriously. But this Old School *vs.* Neo-whatever is just a bunch of silly hype.

---

30 Gertrude Stein, *Everybody's Autobiography,* (New York: Random House, 1937)

If you don't have a good story, something to be WOMed or if the demographics aren't there (many demographics won't respond to WOM)—then don't use it.

The danger of and possible swan song of WOM: People will eventually see shills coming, will recognize shill-talk, shill blogs—and ignore it all.

In March of the next year, Jack Trout had something to say about WOMM marketing in *Forbes*:

How many people really want to chatter about products? Do you really want to talk about your toothpaste or your toilet paper . . . ? This all brings me to my word-of-mouth on word-of-mouth marketing. It's not the next big thing. It's just another tool in your arsenal. If you have a way to get your strategy or point of difference talked about by your customers and prospects, that's terrific. It will help, but you're going to have to surround it with a lot of other effort, including, if you'll pardon the expression, advertising. You just can't buy mouths the way you can buy media. And mouths can stop talking |about you in a heartbeat once something else comes along to talk about.

—Jack Trout, *Forbes*[31]

Eight months later David Jones jumps in:

We've got to stop thinking that consumer-generated content is an idea. It isn't. It is a phenomenon. . . . The problem with relying on communications created by regular Joes . . . is that they rarely create content with your brand strategy in their pocket. Our industry cannot delegate the creation of brilliant ideas to consumers.

—David Jones, Euro RSCG Worldwide[32]

I repeat: *I am not anti-WOM marketing.* I understand the power and influence of the internet.

---

31 Jack Trout, "Is Word of Mouth All It's Cracked Up to Be?" *Forbes Magazine*, March 7, 2006
32 Lisa Sanders, "Ignore the Research and Trust Your Gut," *Advertising Age*, November 2, 2006

But remember this: Advertising didn't die with the invention of the telephone.

New Research and Personality Profiling

Over the last few years there have been a half dozen or so Baby Boomer research reports brandished by major and not-so-major companies and marketing outfits.

I like research. I tend to pour over it. One reason I like it (actually, love it) is because lately it's been retroactively confirming what I've been saying over the last four years in articles about marketing and advertising to Baby Boomers and in this book. A few examples include:

> Nearly one-quarter of U.S. baby-boomers are insulted by the advertising messages that companies are sending them, according to a new study. More than 65% say they are less likely to purchase the product if an ad offends them. Nearly half believed that there was little truth in advertising.
>
> The findings emerged from a study of 30,000 people, aged 42 and over, conducted by Focalyst, a joint venture between Kantar, the WPP advertising group, and AARP.
>
> New insights from Focalyst: 60% wish ads had more real information, suggesting that America's advertising industry may be missing the mark in targeting the most affluent generation in U.S. history.
>
> —*The Focalyst View*[33]

And from a review of the first edition of this book (June, 2005):

> As a member of the generation myself, I now know why so many advertisements leave me cold. I thought it was just me, but after reading *Advertising to Baby Boomers*, I now put the blame squarely where it belongs. Boomers like facts . . . Nyren advises marketers against overselling to Boomers with "blatant

---

33 "The Focalyst View," *Focalyst.com*, September 2006

huckstersim and ballyhoo. You can amuse, but don't assume.
Give us the facts."
— Dr. Joyce M. Wolburg, *Journal of Consumer Marketing*[34]

More from and about the Focalyst survey:

Boomers are still among the consumer groups most prone to
being mythologized by marketers. And one of the most endur-
ing conventional wisdoms is that the 50+ crowd is so brand-
loyal and averse to change that it's not worth the investment
to try to win them over to a new brand.

Dead wrong, according to several speakers at the Focalyst
Executive Forum: Innovations and Insights in Reaching
Boomers and Older Consumers . . . 68 percent of boomers say
that they research various brands and have no trouble switch-
ing brands.
— Karlene Lukovitz, *MediaPost Marketing Daily*[35]

And from the same review by Dr. Wolburg:

A second favorite excuse of agencies is: Baby Boomers don't
change brands. Nyren dismantles this excuse nicely with examples of brand switching, and he further acknowledges that in
cases where loyalty to a brand does exist, marketers who do
not target Boomers give them no reason to change. He maintains that if Boomers like a product they will buy it, endorse
it among their friends, and if it is important enough, they will
make it part of their lives.
— *Journal of Consumer Marketing*[36]

Research for the most part is numbers, focus and control-group
surveys, surveys sent to people who may or may not fill them out and
return them. It's all great, all interesting, illuminating, and important.

34 Dr. Joyce M. Wolburg, Review of *Advertising to Baby Boomers*, *Journal of Consumer Marketing*, Vol 23, Issue 3, October 2006

35 Karlene Lukovitz, "We Knew Boomers Are Into Sex—But Brand Switching?" *MediaPost Marketing Daily*, September 29, 2006

36 Dr. Joyce M. Wolburg, Review of *Advertising to Baby Boomers*, *Journal of Consumer Marketing*, Vol 23, Issue 3, October 2006

But there are sticky issues when interpreting marketing data. Brent Green talks about one recent survey and the publicized results:

> What ——— does not share with us is the survey design, the actual questions posed to survey respondents, the order in which the questions were posed, or how the questions were framed by interviewers. There are many ways that surveys can be designed and scripted to create self-fulfilling prophesies.
>
> —Brent Green, *Boomers* blog[37]

There are many ways of fashioning raw data into something usable. However, I wonder about the wisdom of personality profiling. What good does it really do for a marketer?

> Articles (in recent marketing magazines and press releases) inevitably contain the revelation that it is possible to divide older people into strange tribal groups. They are given names like the sophisticated "Astute Cosmopolitans" and the boring "Thrifty Traditionalists." Other than the amusement value, why are consumers . . . dissected into so many weird sounding segments?
>
> —Dick Stroud, *Millennium's Circus Newsletter*[38]

> Now that most marketers have realized that today's Boomer Consumers are still worthy of their attention, they are scrambling to find the best segmentation scheme. . . . The problem, of course, is that most segmentation schemes have little or no value to most marketers. . . . Recently we've seen a slew of new segmentation schemes based on research by a variety of organizations. (One) identified five segments with names like *Empowered Trailblazers, Wealth-Builders, Leisure Lifers, Anxious Idealists.* . . . Another firm identified 24 segments. (Another identified six.)
>
> —Matt Thornhill, *Boomer Marketing News*[39]

---

37 http://boomers.typepad.com/

38 Dick Stroud, "Marketing to the Over-Fifties," *Circus Newsletter,* April 2006

39 Matt Thornhill, "Segment Schmegment," *Boomer Marketing News,* Vol 1, Number 2, November 2006

Let's say a research firm comes out with all sorts of fun data and happily declares that there are twelve Baby Boomer personality types. (I picked twelve because the whole thing reminds me of astrology.). Instead of defining the personality types, I'll simply refer to them as numbers—so this exercise doesn't get too convoluted.

I want to turn the research/survey process inside out, upside down, and backwards. Sure, my example below is *not the way research surveys are constructed*. But humor me. I'm more interested in peeling away the sources of most surveys, and explaining why they do not lend themselves to personality profiling. Now, for the fun part:

Let's say you've decided that Sally Boomer is your target market. Sally is 55, married, with adult children and two grandchildren. Sally has a big chunk of disposable income because she and her husband have worked for most of their adult lives.

Oddly enough, Sally B. is a friend of mine. I've known her since high school. If you ask me, I'd tell you that Sally has changed through the years, but is pretty much personality type #4, with a smidgeon of #10.

If you were to ask Sally's husband which personality type Sally is, he would tell you she's #2, but she'd probably tell you that she's #7. For example, her husband would say that Sally thinks she's thrifty—but he thinks she's actually is quite the spendthrift. While she doesn't buy a lot of small, dumb things, she saves up and buys big, dumb things. Her husband also would say that Sally thinks she is selfish and self-centered, and berates herself for this, even though she spends a chunk of her free time doing volunteer work. Her husband doesn't think Sally is selfish at all.

Sally has a brother and sister. They have their own opinion of what personality types Sally is. And Sally's three kids—well, we won't ask. At the moment, two of them are not too happy with their mother. If we were to ask them, they would probably say that there should be a #13 on the personality profile list: "Evil Mom." Sally's grandchildren adore her, however. But they are only seven, ten, and twelve years old, so we won't quiz them about Sally. They simply adore her. Sally spoils them, even though she doesn't think she does.

Now it's time for Sally to weigh in. Sally says she's definitely #6, but is also a little bit of #11. However, the next morning, after two cups of coffee and a fight on the phone with one of her daughters about spoiling the grandchildren, she crosses out #6 and circles #3. That's what she feels like at the moment: #3.

Sally went to a psychologist a few years ago—nothing serious, just to work out a few problems. If we were to ask the psychologist what personality type Sally is, we'd have a different take on Sally Boomer. As far as the psychologist can tell (and this certainly isn't a professional diagnosis, as personality types are not pathological), Sally is a #5.

Three days later Sally digs up the survey under a pile of newspapers (she's been meaning to send it in, but forgot—and now is glad she hadn't) and takes a look at it. She crosses out #3 and circles #8.

So it's time to come up with a marketing plan and ad campaign targeting Sally Boomer. Which Sally do you target? And even if by some magical formula you find out what personality type Sally *really* is, do you target who Sally really is or who she *thinks* she is? By the time you've crunched the survey, Sally, who remembers the survey—and in fact, thinks about it every now and then because she took it so seriously has changed her mind about who she is. She's not only made up with her daughters, but recently, for no apparent reason, has started to buy really dumb little things for herself and her grandchildren. Sally thinks that she's become some sort of spendthrift. Perhaps the idea was put in her head because of the survey. She'd never really thought about whether or not she was a spendthrift. And, after talking to her husband and her children and some of her friends about the survey, and hearing what they think her personality types are, she's not convinced that she answered the questionnaire truthfully. How she wishes she could get that survey back so she could fill it out again.

Let me tell you about Chuck Boomer. I've been described as self-less and self-obsessed, traditional and experimental, panicky and secure, a spendthrift and stingy, pompous and humble, deeply concerned about the human condition and embarrassingly shallow, pragmatic and altruistic, honest and unctuous, noble and petty, cheery and curmudgeonly, fearless and cowardly, lazy and industrious.

And guess what. They're all right. I'm all of those things. Now, go ahead and sell me something.

There are better ways interpreting data and ultimately slicing and dicing cohorts than personality profiling.

The Me Generation Becomes the We Generation

Baby Boomers are commonly thought to be the most self-absorbed generation in American history. . . . Yet, ultimately, the bad rap might prove to be undeserved. . . . The emerging model embraces personal growth, giving back and continued employment. These hallmarks of the new retirement have the potential to reshape the economy and society to everyone's benefit.

Will boomers really give something back? They already are. Nationally, boomers (33%) have higher volunteer rates than either seniors (24%) or young adults (24%), reports the Corporation for National and Community Service. This is the most schooled and traveled generation in history. . . . The challenge is not, as many have argued, how to pay for an aging society. It's how to harness the skills of a vast, willing and able new crop of maturing Americans who want to stay in the game longer, give something back and help cure society's ills.

—Daniel J. Kadlec, *USA Today*[40]

The information above usually shocks people. No big surprise if you've done some research, not on Baby Boomers, but on the accepted constructs of human aging. Shakespeare talks about the Seven Ages of Man. Albert Maslow's Hierarchy of Needs attempts to codify it.

---

40 Daniel J. Kadlec, "*Me* Generation becomes *We* Generation," *USA Today,* August 2, 2006

David Wolfe writes eloquently about it in his book *Ageless Marketing*. Philosophers, historians, writers, biographers, and anybody with even a passing knowledge of sociology and psychology know that a person's needs, wants, and interests change through the years.

Baby Boomers were stigmatized when we were in and around our twenties, early thirties. Sure, we were "me" back then. Barring tragedies like war and all sorts of catastrophes similarly horrifying, most young adults are "me, me, me," self-obsessed to the *nth* degree. They have to be. It's the period for figuring out who you are, making something of yourself, which requires being mostly selfish or self-obsessed. Not such a bad path to take when you're young and getting your bearings. If you don't, you might not survive. Some of us went a bit overboard and didn't survive, but it was a small percentage.

What happened is that there were so many of us in the 1970s when the term "me generation" was coined that it ended up being the zeitgeist of the industrialized world. This image stereotype followed us. As we hit our late thirties, forties, fifties, and now some of us banging into our sixties, we were too busy to bother about this silly "branding" of ourselves.

Today, Baby Boomers are two or three times removed from being a "me" generation. What constitutes self-actualization when you are twenty-five is different than when you are fifty-five. In your twenties, you think of yourself as the picture. As you get older, you see yourself more and more as a picture piece that is part of a bigger picture.

Talk to some folks in their twenties or thirties. They are now in that "me" stage. It's healthy and smart for them to be so. I was just like them thirty years ago, and get a big bang out of them. I, admire their boundless creativity, energy, and self-obsession. These "me" generation twentysomethings today will become a "we" generation' in thirty years.

There's nothing new here. I came up with none of this. Take it up with Mr. Shakespeare or Professor Maslow if you have any issues with the above information.

What is different about Baby Boomers is a middle-age mindset, supercharged with medical advances which will, for the most part, keep us active and alert.

> Baby boomers are a generation like no other. Socially conscious, revolutionary and taboo-shattering, these Americans continue to challenge the status quo, even as the first wave enters their "golden years.". . . It's no surprise that as Boomers have aged, their trend-setting beliefs have deeply impacted their personal lives, careers, retirement decisions and relationships with the world around them. . . . As healthcare improves, so do the lives of Boomer Americans. . . . (They) will have more years to contribute to society and accomplish their life goals than any previous generation. In fact, most Boomers plan to continue working well into their 60s and 70s. . . . The Boomer legacy will leave behind a distinct set of values, but most notably inspiring, inviting, informing and spirited lives. For them and generations to follow, a new life begins at 50. Boomers are showing America how to live without restraints, armed with the confidence to look into the future and to continue building fulfilling lives.
>
> —*AXcess News* [41]

Our interests, needs, and wants in middle age aren't different than previous generations. What we *will* be able to do is attack these interests, needs, and wants with different attitudes and physical capabilities. There have always been a small percentage of people in all generations who kept going, never disengaged, and continued to be creative, energized, and involved. For us, this combustible combination of qualities is the rule, not the exception. Baby Boomers have embraced the "age" we are in, but have formed a fresh ethos.

> Is 50 the new 30? 60 the new 40? No. It's better than that: Sixty is the new 60.
>
> —Gail Sheehy [42]

---

41 "Baby Boomers Redefine Aging in the New Millennium," editorial, *AXcess News*, May 19, 2006

42 Jada Yuan, "Passage Marker: Gail Sheehy," *New York Magazine*, February 20, 2006

Our later stage "ages" have been and will be extended and infused with mental and physical vitality. Watch out. We'll be causing even more trouble over the next twenty-five years.

And if you market or advertise to us, remember that we're still meaningfully engaged—so you'd better do something meaningful to engage us.

Baby Boomers Jumping Over Fences ...

After finishing the first edition of this book and then speaking at a number of conferences, doing private consulting on the road or over the phone, yacking it up during newspaper and magazine interviews and on numerous radio and television shows (and spending time blogging, of course), it certainly seems to me as if I'm the penultimate self-obsessed Baby Boomer. This is an understatement, and the irony doesn't escape me.

But something happened not long into this recent whirlwind of consulting and speaking. I realized that the message was sound, but it needed a caveat. My fear was that many people, especially after a day-long business conference focused solely on marketing to Baby Boomers, probably went back to their hotel rooms, plopped their heads on their pillows, closed their eyes—and to get to sleep they would start counting Baby Boomers jumping over fences.

And I know it was true. I could always tell by follow-up meetings and telephone calls.

Repeating what I said at the beginning of this Afterward: *Instead of using the sensibilities required for reaching this diverse market, ad agencies are taking the easy way out by trying to sell their target market to their target market.* I guess we evangelists are a bit to blame. We sell "Baby Boomers" to the marketing, advertising, and media industries—and they *resell* them.

You already know what I'm about to say. You learned in it Marketing & Advertising 101. But sometimes it's easy to forget the obvious. I forget it sometimes . . .

When you rev up to create a campaign for any demographic, put the target market on the back burner on the lowest setting. On low.

The lowest. It's the product or service that needs to be in front, on high.

Consumers, in this case tens of millions of Baby Boomers, don't care if you think they are a Baby Boomer. They're not walking around wondering how you are going to reach them with your marketing and advertising. They don't care whether or not what I say is smart or dumb, right or wrong. They don't care about my book, or any marketing books, or any marketing pundits—or care about you and your marketing and advertising campaigns. They don't care or think about any of it. All you can hope is that they may be interested in your product or service.

They watch a commercial and even if they like it, they are waiting for it to end. They flip the page in a magazine, stare, and even before focusing they have their fingers readied to turn the page. They are fiddling with their mouse as they scan the screen. They are driving and (we all hope) are paying attention to the road as they listen to your radio spot.

You have to position your offering so they find it inviting. You must make them curious. And you invite them and make them curious by speaking their language. If the message is jarring and foreign to them, if they can't "relate" to it, it becomes the clutter everybody talks about cutting through. And if it's insulting—if it's "You're a Baby Boomer so here's the product for you!"—well, let's hope they're not listening, and are only paying attention to the product.

"Cutting through the clutter." That phrase is getting old. "We're going to do a commercial, a print ad, a marketing campaign that will cut through the clutter!" The irony I find with many campaigns today is that the "clutter" is *in the commercials*. What dry muck I have to sit through just to find out that there's there is nothing there.

You are trying to reach people in their late forties, fifties, sixties. There is a certain style of advertising Baby Boomers grew up with and feel comfortable with. Look at commercials from the late 1950s through the middle 1970s. Look at magazine ads from that period. Something was going on there that isn't going on today. Don't focus on the obvious retro bric-a-brac—cull the intelligence and immediacy inherent in many of those campaigns. They don't insult the consumer or the product. They make fun of consumers and even the products sometimes, but they don't make you feel like you're an idiot.

> Over 50s do retain a sense of humor. Some data suggests that this group is less likely to enjoy humorous ads, but we expect this may actually reflect the fact that too often ads are targeted at—and created by—younger people, whose humor may be offensive or irrelevant to an older target.
>
> —Nigel Hollis, Millward Brown[43]

Create intelligent, witty, direct campaigns. Then combine this with a more mature sensibility.

But even after listening to me (among others) prattle on about marketing to Baby Boomers, ultimately, when you sit down and get ready to get to work, forget everything we've said. It'll all still be there. Just purposely ignore it.

Then focus on the product.

---

43 Nigel Hollis, "Over Fifty But Not Over the Hill," *Straight Talk with Nigel Hollis*, www.mb-blog.com, November 28, 2006

INDEX

ABOUT THE AUTHOR

CHUCK NYREN is an award-winning advertising video producer, creative strategist, consultant, and copywriter focusing on The Baby Boomer market.

Chuck has been in advertising since before he was born—a true "'Madison Avenue Baby.'" His grandfather Sid Schwinn was one of the advertising greats of the Twenties, Thirties, and Forties. Over fifty years ago Mr. Schwinn penned *The Simple Simon Stories* about advertising. It is still on the recommended reading lists of many college and university advertising and marketing courses. Chuck's mother was a copywriter, and his father was V.P. of Programming for a major advertising agency. While Chuck doesn't want anybody reading this to feel aesthetically deprived or culturally deficient, he often reveals that he is one of only a handful of people ever to see the original 15-minute pilot for *The Munsters*.

Being a true 60s teenager, Chuck at first rebelled against advertising. He has been in and out of the industry for thirty-five years. Like most lives, his has been filled with ups and downs, successes and failures, clarities and ambiguities. Now he has reformed, seen the light, and returned to the fold. Copywriting, creative strategy, consulting, and penning popular, worldwide syndicated columns about advertising to Baby Boomers is his calling.

Chuck has been a consultant for advertising and marketing agencies and companies with products for the 40+ Market, including Ignite Ventures, BooM Magazine, Mary Furlong & Associates, AARP, NAHB, GRAND Magazine, Harris Interactive, AstraZeneca, WPP's Commonhealth, and The Omnicom Group. He is a member/consultant (Advertising/40+Market) with The Faith Popcorn BrainReserve TalentBank, a leading trend forecasting marketing firm.

Through the years he has written copy and/or has been a creative strategist for Microsoft, Mackie Designs, and various international professional audio manufacturers, many small Seattle-based ad agencies and companies, and numerous television and radio stations from coast to coast. Chuck has won three International Competition Cindy® Awards (Cinema in Industry), two Gold and one Silver.

He has been interviewed by *The New York Times, The Los Angeles Times, The Dallas Morning News, The Hartford Courant, The Philadelphia Inquirer, The Milwaukee Journal Sentinel, BusinessWeek*, CBS *MarketWatch, Tiempos Del Mundo*, KIRO-AM (Seattle), WBIX (Boston), *Advertising Age*'s *The Advertising Show, Selling to Seniors, Counselor* and *Advantages* magazines (The Advertising Specialty Institute), *U.S. News & World Report, The Franchise Times, Confectioner Magazine, Street & Smith's Sports Business Journal*, and many other newspapers, magazines and radio programs worldwide. Chuck is a talking head on an episode of The History Channel/AARP 2006–2007 television series *Our Generation.*

Mr. Nyren's fiction has been published in various literary journals, short story anthologies, and "ezines" including *Grandfathers are Gold* (Simon & Schuster), *SpinDrifter, The Satire Quarterly, The Hot Flash Cafe, Eclectica*—and on coffee cans in Portland, Oregon. His one-act plays are staged nationwide a half-dozen or so times a year.

Chuck lives in Snohomish, Washington. One of his favorite activities is writing about himself in the third person.